BATMAN Detective No. 27

writer: **MICHAEL USLAN**

artist: **PETER SNEJBJERG**

letterer: **KURT HATHAWAY**

colorist & separator: **LEE LOUGHRIDGE**

BATMAN created by **BOB KANE**

BATMAN: DETECTIVE #27. PUBLISHED BY DC COMICS, 1700 BROADWAY, NEW YORK, NY 10019.
COPYRIGHT © 2003 DC COMICS. ALL RIGHTS RESERVED. ALL CHARACTERS FEATURED IN THIS
ISSUE, THE DISTINCTIVE LIKENESSES THEREOF AND RELATED INDICIA ARE TRADEMARKS OF
DC COMICS. THE STORIES, CHARACTERS AND INCIDENTS MENTIONED IN THIS MAGAZINE ARE
ENTIRELY FICTIONAL. DC COMICS DOES NOT READ OR ACCEPT UNSOLICITED SUBMISSIONS
OF IDEAS, STORIES OR ARTWORK. DC COMICS, A WARNER BROS. ENTERTAINMENT COMPANY.
PRINTED IN CANADA.
HARDCOVER ISBN: 1-4012-0185-7
SOFTCOVER ISBN: 1-4012-0107-5
COVER DESIGN: TERRY MARKS

ACT ONE

APRIL, 1865...WASHINGTON, DC... FROM THE ASHES OF ATLANTA TO THE BLOOD-SOAKED BLADES OF GETTYSBURG GRASS, FROM APPOMATTOX COURT HOUSE TO FORD'S THEATRE...THE AIR IS THICK WITH *FEAR*...

CALM YOURSELF, *MR. PINKERTON.* THE LAST THING I NEED IS TO BE THE DEATH OF YOU.

WE'VE KNOWN EACH OTHER MUCH TOO LONG TO MINCE WORDS, MR. PRESIDENT. I WILL *NOT* HAVE YOU GOING TO *FORD'S THEATRE* TONIGHT!

THE ADDRESS IS 1600 PENNSYLVANIA AVENUE, BUT NORTHERNERS SIMPLY REFER TO IT AS "THE PRESIDENT'S HOUSE"...

DON'T *YOU* TELL MY HUSBAND WHAT HE *IS* OR IS *NOT* TO DO, SIR! HE IS YOUR *PRESIDENT*, AND I SAY WE *ARE* ATTENDING THE THEATRE TONIGHT!

CALM DOWN, MOTHER. HE MEANS WELL.

ABE...YOU BROUGHT ME TO WASHINGTON TO FORM A *SECRET SERVICE* TO HANDLE YOUR SECURITY--

AFTER YOU THWARTED THE ASSASSINATION ATTEMPT ON ME IN 1861, WHO *ELSE* WOULD I TRUST WITH MY LIFE, ALLAN?

THEN HEAR ME *NOW!* THE SECRET SERVICE HAS *NO JURISDICTION* OVER WASHINGTON'S CITY SECURITY.

I *DON'T* WANT YOU ABOUT TOWN WITHOUT *OUR* PROTECTION!

POPPYCOCK! I'LL NOT BE DENIED AN EVENING OF THEATRE BY YOU OR *ANYONE!* DO YOU *HEAR* ME, SIR? IF *NOT*, PERHAPS THEN IF I *SCREAM?*

AAIEEE!

THAT'S QUITE ENOUGH, MOTHER. MY DECISION IS MADE.

WE GO TO THE THEATRE TONIGHT.

YET ONE *MORE* MOMENT OF MAN'S INHUMANITY TOWARD MAN, FROZEN IN TIME...

LATER, IN THE DIM GASLIGHT OF THE PRESIDENT'S OFFICE, A SOLITARY FIGURE MOURNS FOR HIS FRIEND...AND FOR WHAT *MIGHT* HAVE BEEN...

APRIL, 1929...GOTHAM CITY...AN EVENING OF SWASHBUCKLING CELLULOID...FOLLOWED BY A STROLL HOME THROUGH PARK ROW...AS A BOY'S EXCITEMENT EVAPORATES INTO A CLOUD OF CONFUSION...AND CONFUSION CONDENSES INTO *FEAR*...

EXTRY! EXTRY! READALLABOUTIT! "LINCOLN'S DEATH CHAIR BOUGHT BY HENRY FORD!"

LOOK HOW THIS NEIGHBORHOOD'S DETERIORATING, TOM. SOMEBODY SHOULD DO SOMETHING ABOUT IT! IT'S A CRIME!

I'LL MAKE SOME CALLS...SEND SOME CHECKS.

AREN'T YOU GLAD I MADE YOU SEE THIS MOVIE TONIGHT? WASN'T IT THE CAT'S MEOW?

TOM, THERE'S SOMEONE FOLLOWING US!

4

YOU HAVE YOUR PAPERS AND YOUR MONEY. WHEN THE MAURITANIA DOCKS IN LIVERPOOL—

I KNOW! I KNOW! YOUR DETECTIVE FRIEND FROM SCOTLAND YARD WILL MEET ME AND DRIVE ME TO THE SCHOOL IN LONDON.

OXFORD!

WHATEVER...

AND KEEP IN MIND, YOUR FATHER'S SERVICE CHUM FROM *THE WORLD WAR* WILL ACCOMPANY YOU TO THE *ORIENT* WHEN YOU—

I KNOW!

AND WRITE ME EACH AND EVERY DAY, YOUNG MAN!

I WILL!

DON'T FORGET TO—

I WON'T!

"LIFE": A SERIES OF UNFOLDING EVENTS STRUNG TOGETHER BY A SEEMINGLY ENDLESS PROCESSION OF GOOD-BYES...

THIS *MANUSCRIPT* IS THE REASON I HAVE POURED OUR FINANCIAL RESOURCES INTO SECURING THE LOYALTY AND SERVICES OF THE SOUTH'S MOST BRILLIANT *BOTANISTS,* RESEARCH SCIENTISTS, AND DOCTORS.

WITH CONFEDERATE MONEY HAVING BECOME *VALUELESS,* MEN HAVE BECOME *DESPERATE.* DESPERATION SUPPLANTS PRINCIPLE AND HONOR.

WITHOUT PRINCIPLE AND HONOR, THE HEARTS AND MINDS OF MEN MAY BE BOUGHT BY GOLD...

...*OUR* GOLD!

EXPERIMENTS IN PLANT HYBRIDIZATION

by

Gregor Mendel

THIS UNPUBLISHED WORK BY AN OBSCURE AUSTRIAN *MONK* IS THE KEY TO OUR SUCCESS...*IF* WE EXHIBIT THE PATIENCE OF JOB.

OUR LATE PRESIDENT'S *FAVORITE* BOOK...

...TONIGHT, WITH A DELICIOUS DASH OF IRONY, IT BECOMES YET ANOTHER *WEAPON* IN OUR REIGN OF *TERROR* AGAINST THE *ENEMY!*

JOE MILLER'S JOKE BOOK

AND SO, INSPIRED BY *JOE MILLER,* THE KING OF JOKERS AND RIDDLERS, I POSE THE QUESTION *THE NORTH* WILL ONE DAY BE *FORCED* TO ANSWER...

HAVE YOU EVER DANCED WITH THE DEVIL BY THE PALE MOONLIGHT?

NEW YEAR'S DAY, 1939... GOTHAM CITY'S ROOSEVELT FIELD...A PAN AM CLIPPER ARRIVES FROM THE ORIENT, BRINGING A *CHANGED* BOY BACK TO HIS *VERY* CHANGED HOME...

AND I SIMPLY MUST *CHIDE* THE LAD FOR *WASTING* TIME LEARNING *PARLOUR* TRICKS FROM DR. WAYNE'S OLD WAR CHUM IN THE ORIENT!

"CLOUDING MEN'S MINDS"? INDEED!

TEN YEARS OF *PERFECT* MARKS IN CRIMINOLOGY, EVERY SCIENCE, LANGUAGES, BUSINESS, ENGINEERING, PERSONAL FITNESS, BOXING...

ALFRED!

MASTER BRUCE? MY OH MY! IT *IS*!

Hmmm...EVEN ORIENTAL FIGHTING TECHNIQUES, AUTOMOTIVE REPAIR, MEDITATION, COSTUME DESIGN AND PROP-MAKING!

ALL THAT'S *MISSING* IS "CAREER COUNSELING!" <TSK-TSK> NO FOCUS AT ALL!

SOME CAR! WHEN'D WE GET *THIS* BABY?

"WE" DID NOT. "I" DID. MY VERY *FIRST* AUTOMOBILE!

THAT'S *GREAT,* ALFRED! I'M GLAD MY *FATHER* LEFT YOU ENOUGH MONEY TO HANDLE ALL YOUR NEEDS.

ACTUALLY, MASTER BRUCE, I PURCHASED THIS WITH MY *OWN* MONEY. I'VE EARNED A *TIDY SUM* SINCE YOU'VE BEEN ABROAD.

GUESS I SHOULD HAVE KEPT UP *MORE* WITH OUR CORRESPONDENCE. I'M *NOT* THE GREAT COMMUNICATOR MY *MOTHER* ALWAYS WAS.

YOU STILL THINK OF THEM OFTEN?

NOT A *DAY* GOES BY I HAVEN'T THOUGHT OF MY *MOM*...MY *DAD*... AND...AND THAT NIGHT.

HOME AT *LAST*, MASTER *BRUCE!* WELCOME *BACK!*

"M.D."? ALFRED...WHAT'S COOKING WITH THE *SIGN?*

Alfred Pennyworth, M.D.

WELL, HAD YOU READ ALL MY LETTERS... ≳AHEM≲... YOU WOULD KNOW THAT WITH ALL THESE YEARS AND NO FAMILY TO TEND TO, I ENROLLED IN THE GOTHAM CITY MEDICAL SCHOOL.

AND YOU GOT *IN?* JUST LIKE *THAT?*

≳OOF!≲ THANK GOODNESS YOU SHIPPED ALL YOUR *TRUNKS!*

AND TO ANSWER YOUR RATHER *IMPERTINENT* QUESTION, HAVING A CONNEC- TION TO THE *DOCTOR* WHO BEQUEATHED *MILLIONS OF DOLLARS* TO THE SCHOOL UPON HIS DEATH...*MAY HAVE* BEEN HELPFUL.

I HEARD THEY USED MY *FATHER'S* MONEY TO TURN THE PLACE INTO THE MOST TECHNOLOGICALLY *ADVANCED* HOSPITAL AND RESEARCH FACILITY IN THE COUNTRY.

THAT TRUE, "DR." PENNYWORTH?

QUITE.

I SPECIALIZED IN *FORENSIC* MEDICINE, THINKING THAT WHEN YOU CAME HOME, I COULD *ASSIST* YOU IF YOU WERE *STILL* DETERMINED TO...TO...

I FEEL THEIR *PRESENCE* HERE, ALFRED. IT...IT STILL JUST *HURTS* SO *MUCH*...AND I DON'T EVEN KNOW *HOW* TO AVENGE THEM. *WHAT AM I GOING TO DO?* WHAT WOULD MY *DAD* TELL ME?

I THINK HE'D TELL YOU WE'RE TWO MEN CHANGED *FOREVER* BY ONE TRAGEDY. THEN, HE MIGHT QUOTE EMERSON...

"WHAT LIES *BEHIND* US, AND WHAT LIES *BEFORE* US, ARE TINY MATTERS COMPARED TO WHAT LIES *WITHIN* US."

11

APRIL, 1865...WHAT LIES WITHIN THE BELL TOWER OF THE COLLEGE OF GEORGETOWN IS FESTERING *HATRED*...

TODAY IS *LOST*. BUT IN *74 YEARS*, WE WILL EMERGE THE *VICTORS*! "SURVIVAL OF THE FITTEST."

AND IN THE YEAR *1939* THE KNIGHTS OF THE GOLDEN CIRCLE WILL BE THE FITTEST! THE *SOUTH WILL RISE AGAIN*!

74 YEARS?!! ARE YOU *INSANE*?

YOU THINK OUR *ARMY* CAN RISE AGAIN ANY *FASTER*?

GENTLEMEN, OUR *GOLD* HAS BOUGHT US THE SERVICES OF THE UNDER APPRECIATED GENIUS WHO FIRST REALIZED THE CONCEPT OF "SURVIVAL OF THE FITTEST," THE BRITISH NATURALIST *CHARLES DARWIN*!

AND NOW ONE *MORE* SURPRISE...

THIS EVENING, I RECEIVED *PROOF* THAT CHARLES DARWIN IS, AS WE SPEAK, ENSCONCED IN A DEBATE IN LONDON OVER "NATURAL SELECTION."

APPARENTLY, THERE ARE *TWO* CHARLES DARWINS...

...AND I HAVE, NATURALLY, *SELECTED THIS ONE TO DIE*!

AND WHO *ELSE* COULD INFILTRATE OUR ORGANIZATION TIME AND AGAIN BUT...

ALLAN PINKERTON!

...WHO SHALL *NOW* JOIN HIS FRIEND, MR. LINCOLN, IN *HELL*!

THE *ONLY* SCALAWAGS JOURNEYING TO HELL *THIS* NIGHT ARE BOOTH AND *YOU*, JOSIAH CARR!

K-CHAK!

12

MR. PINKERTON, *SURELY* YOU COMPREHEND THAT IT MATTERS *NOT* IF YOU SHOOT ME DEAD ON THE SPOT? I'VE ALREADY *WON!*

WON? IF YOU BELIEVE THE *BLOOD* OF ABRAHAM LINCOLN ON YOUR HANDS MEANS—

NOTHING! IT MEANS *NOTHING!* OH... ICING ON THE CAKE, PERHAPS...

POW POW POW

CRASH

WHAT AN *ARMY* COULD NOT DO, THE KNIGHTS OF THE GOLDEN CIRCLE *SHALL!* AND *74 YEARS* OF WAITING WILL BE A *SMALL* PRICE TO PAY FOR *ULTIMATE* VICTORY!

THE PLAN HAS BEEN SET INTO MOTION. AND THE MOTION IS NOW *IRREVERSIBLE!*

DON'T BE *RIDICULOUS,* MAN! YOU, ME, AND ALL OUR *CHILDREN* WILL BE LYING IN THE *DUST* IN 74 YEARS!

TRUE... SOME DOCTOR OR PROFESSOR NOT YET BORN WILL TRIGGER *DOOMSDAY* FOR THE NORTH IN *1939.* AND I WILL *NOT* BE ALIVE TO WITNESS IT.

BUT *NO LONGER* IS THIS ABOUT MY *LIFE.* IT IS ABOUT MY *LEGACY...* MY *LASTING* LEGACY!

SO SHOOT ME, MR. PINKERTON! I AM NOW *MORE* VALUABLE TO MY CAUSE AS A *MARTYR* THAN AS A LEADER.

THAT HUGE *TORCH* IN MADISON SQUARE--!

ONCE WE RAISE ENOUGH MONEY, IT WILL TOP FRANCE'S STATUE OF "LIBERTY ENLIGHTENING THE WORLD" IN THE HARBOR!

WE KNOW *MENDEL'S* PAPERS GAVE BIRTH TO THIS *DOOMSDAY PLOT.* BUT WHAT COULD POSSIBLY TAKE *75 YEARS* TO METAMORPHOSE INTO AN UNSTOPPABLE WEAPON OF DEADLY FEAR?

SOME SCIENTIFIC OR MEDICAL "FRANKENSTEIN"? SOME UNCONTROLLABLE NEW *PLAGUE?*

57TH STREET! MY *HOME* IS JUST--

OUR YEARS OF SLEUTHING HAVE LED US TO PLANT *TOXINS.* THAT'S WHY THE KNIGHTS OF THE GOLDEN CIRCLE CONTINUE RECRUITING *BOTANISTS,* AMONG OTHERS.

HERE'S *CENTRAL PARK'S* "POLO GROUNDS." THE POLO TEAM MOVED ON TO GREENER PASTURES, LEAVING THIS TO OUR BASEBALL CLUB, "THE NEW YORK METROPOLITANS." QUITE *THRILLING!*

DRAT IT ALL, TEDDY!

THIS PLOT MAY YET *TOPPLE* A CITY! AND I HARDLY THINK *BASEBALL* WILL GIVE US A CLUE HOW TO *STOP* IT! SO IF I MAY HAVE YOUR *UNDIVIDED* ATTENTION--?

WITH *ALL* DUE RESPECT, MR. PINKERTON, YOU FAIL TO *DESERVE* MY UNDIVIDED ATTENTION, HAVING PROVIDED ME WITH *NO* EXPLANATION OF *WHO* OR *WHAT* IS A "SECRET SOCIETY OF DETECTIVES."

SOUNDS LIKE AN "OLD SLEUTH" *DIME* NOVEL!

TO PROTECT ITS MEMBERSHIP AND PRESERVE ITS ANONYMITY, THE SECRET SOCIETY OF DETECTIVES GIVES EACH INITIATE A NUMBER AND TAKES AWAY HIS NAME.

AND SO, IN ALL SOCIETY CORRESPONDENCE AND CONTACT, I'M SIMPLY "DETECTIVE #1: KATE--"DETECTIVE #2" AND WILLIAM-- "DETECTIVE #3."

WELL, IF IT'S SECRECY YOU DESIRE, YOU MIGHT WANT TO LOWER YOUR VOICE. IN THIS PART OF THE CITY, BETTER FOR A MAN OF NOTABLE MEANS TO WALK SOFTLY AND KEEP HIS WALLET.

I FORMED THIS UNIT TO COUNTER THE KNIGHTS OF THE GOLDEN CIRCLE...EVEN SHOULD IT TAKE THE FULL 75 YEARS TO EXPOSE ITS PLOT AND CORRAL ITS GROWING MEMBERSHIP.

EACH DETECTIVE WE RECRUIT MUST BE THE BEST AND, AS WITH ALL MY "PINKS," BE UNCORRUPTIBLE, UNCOMPROMISING, AND "NEVER SLEEP" ON THE JOB!

WHACK

"WALK SOFTLY," EH?

WHACK WHACK

...ER... AND CARRY A BIG STICK! HA!

21

AS I WAS SAYING, I DON'T WANT MERE DETECTIVES IN THIS ORGANIZATION. I WANT THINKERS AND INNOVATORS OF CRIME-SOLVING TECHNIQUES. MEN LIKE ME.

I ORIGINATED MUG SHOTS, CRIME FILES, AND ISOLATED THE "MODUS OPERANDI" AS A MARKER TO IDENTIFY A SUSPECT.

THEY'RE WITH ME, PATRICK.

AND HOW ARE MAUREEN AND THE GIRLS?

JUST DANDY, MR. ROOSEVELT! AND A GOOD DAY TO YOU, SIR!

...AND BY EXAMINING THE SCENE OF A CRIME, I CAN DETERMINE THE PERPETRATOR, AS WELL AS THE DISPOSITION OF HIS ILL-GOTTEN GAINS.

GREGOR MENDEL'S CABIN IS ON THE "B" DECK. AT LEAST, THAT'S WHAT I PAID FOR.

AND WE APPRECIATE THE CONTRIBUTION FROM YOUR CITY FUND, TEDDY. THIS AFFAIR, AFTER ALL, CONCERNS THE VERY SAFETY OF NEW YORK.

WE'RE SET IN WASHINGTON AND GOTHAM, BUT NEED A KEY OPERATIVE IN NEW YORK.

YOUR TENDER AGE DOESN'T SCARE ME, TEDDY, AS THE WORD IS YOUR SIGHTS ARE ALREADY SET ON THE CITY'S POLICE COMMISSIONER JOB.

YOU'RE A MAN OF ACTION AS WELL AS THOUGHT. YOU UNDERSTAND POLICE WORK. YOU CAN BE NEW YORK'S VERY OWN "ALLAN PINKERTON!"

I'M TRULY HUMBLED YOU THINK ALMOST AS MUCH OF ME AS YOU DO OF YOURSELF!

KNOCK KNOCK

YOUR CITY AND COUNTRY NEED YOU. THUS, THE SECRET SOCIETY OF DETECTIVES NEEDS YOU.

WILL YOU BECOME OUR "DETECTIVE #4"?!

Two roads diverged in a yellow wood,
And sorry I could not travel both
And be one traveler, long I stood
And looked down one as far as I could
To where it bent in the undergrowth;

Then took the other, as just as fair
And having perhaps the better claim,
Because it was grassy and wanted wear;
Though as for that, the passing there
Had worn them really about the same,

And both that morning equally lay
In leaves no step had trodden black
Oh, I kept the first for another day!
Yet knowing how way leads on to way,
I doubted if I should ever come back.

I shall be telling this with a sigh
Somewhere ages and ages hence:
Two roads diverged in a wood, and I--
I took the one less traveled by,
And that has made all the difference.

IT'S LIKE MY *FATHER* WAS SPEAKING TO ME FROM *BEYOND* THE GRAVE.

I KNOW *EXACTLY* WHAT TO DO...STARTING WITH A TRIP TO THE *BANK*.

THE...THE *BANK?* BUT, WHY WOULD--?

NOT AN *HOUR* LATER, IN FASHIONABLE DOWNTOWN GOTHAM CITY, BRUCE WAYNE'S NEW GAMEPLAN IMMEDIATELY *UNRAVELS*...

WHAT?! HOW CAN MY FAMILY'S CASH RESERVES BE SO *DEPLETED?!* WHO SOLD OFF THE STOCK? WHO CASHED THE BONDS?

PLEASE *CALM* YOURSELF, MR. WAYNE!

DR. PENNYWORTH HAD TO COVER YOUR RATHER *EXORBITANT* TUITIONS AND LIVING EXPENSES WHILE YOU WERE ABROAD SO LONG.

EXORBITANT?!! ARE YOU *SERIOUS?*

THE REMAINDER OF THE ESTATE WAS LEFT TO *THE GOTHAM CITY MEDICAL SCHOOL.*

SOMETHING *DOESN'T* ADD UP. IS IT *POSSIBLE* THAT ALFRED'S CAR...MED SCHOOL BILLS...NEW OFFICE...?

NO! I HAVE TO TRUST SOMEONE!

YOU...ER...DON'T BELIEVE THERE WAS ANY FINANCIAL *IMPROPRIETY* BY THE BANK, DO YOU?

SAY! HOW ABOUT A *STEAK*, ALFRED? I'VE BEEN DREAMING OF ONE FOR THE LAST *THREE* YEARS!

EXTRY! EXTRY! READALLABOUTIT! *"CRIMSON AVENGER"* STRIKES AGAIN! *EXTRY!*

HERE'S A *DIME*, KID. KEEP THE CHANGE.

WOW! THANKS, MISTER!

ABSURD! HE DRESSES LIKE YOUR OLD MOVIE HERO, *"ZORRO!"* ALTHOUGH IT *DOES* SAY HE EXPOSED A NEST OF *FIFTH COLUMNISTS* AND BROKE UP A *BUND* MEETING.

I PLAN ON DOING *BETTER.*

HOW? FOLLOWING YOUR *FATHER'S* ADVICE?

WHO IS THE CRIMSON AVENGER?

NO...*TEDDY ROOSEVELT'S.*

25

JULY, 1884...THREE MERE MORTAL MEN MEET...LONG BEFORE HISTORY WILL LABEL THEM *LEGENDS*...

GREGOR MENDEL? I'M MR. PINKERTON. THIS IS MR. ROOSEVELT, WHO CORRESPONDED WITH YOU. *WELCOME TO AMERICA.*

THANK YOU. *BUT* AS I EXPLAINED IN MY LETTERS, I HAVE *LITTLE* TO OFFER.

PLEASE LET *US* BE THE JUDGES OF THAT, BROTHER.

AS I WROTE, I *NEVER* HEARD OF *PROFESSOR CARR* OR HIS *KNIGHTS.* HOWEVER, IN 1864, ONE COPY OF MY WORK-IN-PROGRESS WAS, INDEED, *PURLOINED.*

HOW IN *BLAZES* COULD *CARR* HAVE KNOWN OF YOUR CROSS BREEDING RESEARCH CONDUCTED INSIDE AN AUSTRIAN *MONASTERY?!?*

TRAGICALLY, MR. PINKERTON, EVEN A MONASTERY IS *NOT FREE* OF *SIN.*

WORSE, THE EVIDENCE YOU SENT ME *PROVES* THIS PLOT IS PREDICATED UPON *75 YEARS* OF CROSS BREEDING PARTICULAR *POISONOUS* PLANTS...*MAGNIFYING* THEIR TOXINS TO *UNKNOWN* LEVELS.

YET, LACKING A *DELIVERY* SYSTEM SUFFICIENT TO SPREAD THE *TOXINS* TO *LARGE* URBAN CROWDS, THIS PLOT WILL *FAIL.*

...UNLESS...YOU *DON'T* THINK THEY *ALREADY* POSSESS ONE...DO YOU?!

AMBUSH! TEDDY... WE NEED ASSISTANCE *FAST!*

THIS STEAK IS DELICIOUS!

THE HALLUCINOGENIC EFFECTS OF THE COMBINED "DEVILS" WOULD INCLUDE EXTREME PARANOIA AND PANIC, INDUCING UNCONTROLLABLE FEAR IN THE POPULACE.

END OF CIVILIZED LIVING.

END OF A CITY.

THIS IS THE BREAKTHROUGH WE'VE BEEN SEEKING, GENTLEMEN!

UNFORTUNATELY, I HAVE OTHER PRESSING DUTIES TONIGHT. NEW YORK'S FINEST WILL SEE YOU TO YOUR LODGING AT THE DAKOTA.

WE'LL RESUME OUR EFFORTS AT 8 O'CLOCK IN MY OFFICE.

BY THEN, I HOPE THE POLICE WILL HAVE BOTH HYDE AND DR. JEKYLL IN CUSTODY.

ANY PROGRESS?

I THINK BETWEEN BROTHER GREGOR AND YOUR BOSS, THIS CASE MAY BE CRACKED BY TOMORROW!

DID YOU TWO HAVE DINNER? YOU DON'T WANT TO MISS THE FOOD HERE!

THE CHEF, JOHNNY, CAME OUT AND OFFERED TO COOK US STEAKS.

MY MOUTH'S ALREADY WATERING!

THE CHEF IS CHARLES, NOT JOHNNY! 260? GRAYING HAIR?

150...BLOND... SOUTHERN ACCENT...?

THE KITCHEN! QUICKLY!

OH, GOD! THAT'S CHEF CHARLES, I PRESUME. BUT WHO'S HE?

CHARLES DELMONICO. ..THE OWNER. AND I GUARANTEE IT WAS NO HEART ATTACK THAT DID IN EITHER OF THEM! MENDEL WAS RIGHT! IT'S GOT TO BE DATURA!

WHAT ABOUT MY FATHER?!

FATHER! NO!

MY GOD! WE *FAILED* HIM!

DAMN! I'LL GET THE *POLICE* AFTER THE KILLER WILLIAM DESCRIBED.

IT'S UNGODLY! SUMMON YOUR FORENSIC *PATHOLOGISTS* TO--

NO! WE ALREADY *KNOW* IT WAS A MULTIPLE *MURDER!*

BETTER TO LET THEIR DEATHS BE ANNOUNCED AS *NATURAL.* THAT WILL KEEP THE *KNIGHTS* WALLOWING IN *UNCERTAINTY* WHILE WE HUNT THEM DOWN.

HOW DO WE DO THAT, TEDDY? *LOOK* AT THEM!

WE SIMPLY LEAVE THE *CHEF* HERE. HE WAS STRICKEN AT WORK, YES?

AND WE CARRY *DELMONICO* TO HIS PRIVATE QUARTERS UPSTAIRS WHERE, COINCIDENTALLY, HE SUCCUMBED THIS SAME NIGHT.

THEN, WE *SECRETLY* PLACE *MENDEL'S* BODY ON THE NEXT *STEAMSHIP* HOME. THE STEWARD WILL *ASSUME* HE DIED IN HIS SLEEP.

AND MY *FATHER?*

A DEATH BY *NATURAL CAUSES* ON BOARD A PULLMAN CAR TO CHICAGO.

TEDDY...THERE'S *WRITING* ON MY FATHER'S NAPKIN.

AND ON MENDEL'S, ALSO!

DID YOU EVER DANCE WITH THE DEVIL IN THE PALE MOON...

DID YOU EVER DANCE WITH THE DEVIL IN THE PALE MOONLIGHT?

WE NEED *MORE* RECRUITS.

AND TIME IS RUNNING OUT.

GOD *HELP* US!

CARL SANDBURG WROTE ABOUT CHICAGO, BUT, *TRAGICALLY*, HIS WORDS ALSO DESCRIBE *GOTHAM CITY* IN MAY, 1939...

"OF MY CITY THE WORST THAT MEN WILL EVER SAY IS THIS: YOU TOOK LITTLE CHILDREN AWAY FROM THE SUN AND THE DEW, AND THE GLIMMERS THAT PLAYED IN THE GRASS UNDER THE GREAT SKY, AND THE RECKLESS RAIN..."

DAD'S STUDY... *FIRST* ROOM HERE THAT DOESN'T FEEL *SMALLER* NOW... WAS IT REALLY A *LIFETIME* AGO I PLAYED UNDER THAT DESK?

I'M OBSESSING ABOUT *ALFRED*...*CAN'T* HELP IT. HE HAD THE AUTHORITY TO DRAW DOWN FUNDS HE CLAIMED HE NEEDED TO PAY MY EXPENSES.

EVEN IF ALFRED *DIVERTED* THOSE FUNDS TO *HIMSELF*, DAD'S ESTATE HAS *STILL* LEFT ME INCREDIBLY WEALTHY...*BEYOND* ALL MY DREAMS.

I'M READY TO DO WHAT I *HAVE* TO DO...BUT FIRST I MUST HAVE A *DISGUISE*.

CRIMINALS ARE A SUPERSTITIOUS, COWARDLY LOT, SO MY DISGUISE MUST BE ABLE TO STRIKE TERROR INTO THEIR HEARTS. I MUST BE A CREATURE OF THE NIGHT. BLACK, TERRIBLE...A...A...

DING DONG

COMING!

CRACK

STUPID BIRD!

CLICK

HELLO, ALFRED.

MR. TRAVIS! IT'S BEEN *AGES,* SIR. VERY NICE TO SEE YOU.

MASTER BRUCE, DO YOU REMEMBER YOUR *FATHER'S* FRIEND *LEE TRAVIS?* MR. TRAVIS PUBLISHES *"THE DAILY GLOBE LEADER."*

"ALL THE NEWS THAT'S *'LEFT'* TO PRINT"? GOTHAM'S LEADING *LIBERAL* NEWSPAPER? SELLING SUBSCRIPTIONS DOOR-TO-DOOR, MR. TRAVIS?

I *WISH* THERE WAS TIME FOR LEVITY, BRUCE, BUT I NEED TO SPEAK TO YOU *PRIVATELY.* IT'S A MATTER OF GRAVE *URGENCY!*

MR. TRAVIS PUBLICIZED YOUR *FATHER'S* CHARITABLE WORK IN BUILDING AND EQUIPPING *THE GOTHAM CITY MEDICAL SCHOOL.*

I'M *SORRY,* ALFRED, BUT I *MUST* TALK TO BRUCE *ALONE.*

UNFORTUNATELY, I *JUST* RETURNED HOME AFTER TEN YEARS ABROAD, MR. TRAVIS, AND MAY *NOT* BE VERY HELPFUL TO YOU.

IT'S *"LEE."*

AND I KNOW *EXACTLY* WHERE YOU'VE BEEN SINCE *1929.*

YOU *WHAT?* I DON'T FOLLOW.

IN 1864, A SUBVERSIVE CONFEDERATE GROUP, *THE KNIGHTS OF THE GOLDEN CIRCLE,* SET INTO MOTION A "DOOMSDAY PLAN" THAT WOULD *DESTROY* A NORTHERN CITY IN THE YEAR *1939.*

ALLAN PINKERTON, HIMSELF, FORMED A *SECRET SOCIETY OF DETECTIVES* TO RECRUIT THE WORLD'S GREATEST SLEUTHS TO FOIL THE *KNIGHTS* THROUGHOUT THE YEARS.

BUT TIME HAS RUN *OUT!* WE DESPERATELY NEED *YOU* TO JOIN US!

WITHIN THE *HOUR*, A BLINDFOLDED BRUCE WAYNE IS DRIVEN TO A MEETING...THAT *NEVER* OFFICIALLY TAKES PLACE...OF A SOCIETY... THAT *DOESN'T* EXIST... ON THE 103RD FLOOR OF A BUILDING...THAT *SUPPOSEDLY* HAS ONLY *102*...

SORRY FOR THE BLINDFOLD.

S'OKAY. "BLIND-AS-A-BAT" WORKS FOR ME. ARE WE *THERE* YET?

ANONYMITY IS OUR SECURITY, BRUCE. EVERY MEMBER HAS BEEN ASSIGNED A *NUMBER* SINCE *PINKERTON* FIRST BECAME "DETECTIVE #1."

YES, YOU'RE "*THERE*"...

THE *SECRET SOCIETY OF DETECTIVES* WELCOMES YOU, BRUCE WAYNE.

THAT...THAT'S MY *TEACHER* FROM--

FROM THE *ORIENT?* I KNEW YOU'D HAVE TO BE BROUGHT HERE BEFORE YOU'D *BELIEVE* ME.

THEN YOU REALLY *DID* SHADOW ME WHILE I WAS ABROAD FOR TEN YEARS! BUT *WHY?*

SHADOW YOU? HARDLY. WE *CHOSE* YOU, BRUCE... WHEN YOU WERE *TWELVE*.

THE *SOCIETY* ARRANGED YOUR EDUCATION. WE DECIDED THAT WITH THE RIGHT *TRAINING,* YOU COULD GROW UP TO BECOME THE DETECTIVE MOST CAPABLE OF *BREAKING* THIS CASE.

WHAT?! YOU *MANIPULATED* ME? ORCHESTRATED MY *LIFE* WITHOUT MY *KNOWLEDGE?* IMPOSSIBLE!

AND WHY *ME?* WHO COULD MAKE SUCH A *CRITICAL JUDGMENT* ABOUT A YOUNG BOY? WHO WOULD KNOW SO *MUCH* ABOUT ME THAT--OMIGOD!

ALFRED?!

WE PREFER... "DETECTIVE #25!"

AND, YES, "THE BUTLER DID IT!"

I ALWAYS WANTED TO SAY THAT!

YOU *MUST* UNDERSTAND. I HAD *YOUR* BEST INTERESTS AT HEART. I KNEW THAT AT ONLY *TWELVE*, YOU WERE ALREADY *COMMITTED* TO YOUR MISSION.

NO ONE ELSE ON EARTH UNDERSTOOD YOU...HAD *INSIGHT* INTO YOUR NIGHTMARE...YOUR *OBSESSION*.

I SAW YOUR CHILD-HOOD *SACRIFICED* ON AN ALTAR OF BLOOD-STAINED CONCRETE.

AND MAYBE...JUST *MAYBE*...PACKING ME OFF FOR *TEN YEARS* OPENED A CLEAR PATH TO MY FATHER'S FORTUNE FOR *YOU* AND YOUR "JUSTICE SOCIETY" HERE.

"SECRET." SECRET SOCIETY.

WHATEVER!

SO YOU CONTACTED *LEE TRAVIS*, AND THESE BOYS PLANNED WHAT I WOULD AND *WOULDN'T* LEARN?

HOW WONDERFULLY *NIETZSCHEAN!* SOUNDS LIKE THE *HOOEY* I HEARD WHILE STUDYING IN *BERLIN*.

YOUR *EMOTIONS* OVERRULE THE MORE *OBVIOUS* DEDUCTION, BRUCE. *ALFRED* BROUGHT *ME* INTO THE SOCIETY, *NOT VICE VERSA!* I'M DETECTIVE #26!

ALFRED PENNYWORTH HAS BEEN A *MASTER DETECTIVE* FOR SCOTLAND YARD SINCE THE GREAT WAR!

ALFRED... WHAT--?!

AS MR. TRAVIS EXPLAINED EN ROUTE, *THE SECRET SOCIETY* MONITORS ANY *DOCTOR, PROFESSOR* OR *BOTANIST* SHOWING A *SUDDEN RISE* IN *PERSONAL WEALTH...* A POSSIBLE SIGN OF *RECRUITMENT* BY *THE KNIGHTS.*

WHAT COULD THAT *POSSIBLY* HAVE TO DO WITH--?

DR. THOMAS WAYNE'S FORTUNE *AUTOMATICALLY* MADE HIM A *SUSPECT.* I WAS SENT TO GOTHAM TO DETERMINE THE *SOURCE* OF HIS MONEY.

WHO THE HELL *ARE* YOU?! I NO LONGER HAVE A *CLUE!*

YOU *INFILTRATED* MY FAMILY TO *SPY* ON MY *FATHER...* A MAN WHO CONSIDERED YOU A *FRIEND* AND PROVIDED FOR YOU IN HIS *WILL?!*

ALL MY DAD WAS GUILTY OF WAS *PHILANTHROPY.* HE GAVE HIS MONEY TO THE MED SCHOOL, *NOT* THE *KNIGHTS!* THE ONLY ONE *DISHONEST* WAS YOU!

MY FEELINGS FOR YOU AND YOUR PARENTS WERE *GENUINE.*

I UNCOVERED *NO EVIDENCE* AGAINST *DR. WAYNE* AND WAS ABOUT TO *CONFESS* MY IDENTITY TO THEM WHEN...WHEN--

NONE OF THIS MATTERS! THE *DOOMSDAY PLOT'S* A LOT MORE IMPORTANT THAN YOUR FAMILY SPAT!

SO LET'S CUT TO THE CHASE. WAYNE...WE NEED YOUR HELP. YOU *IN* OR *NOT?*

YOU BOYS PICKED THE *WRONG* GUY TO BE YOUR TRAINED *MONKEY!*

THAT SAID, I BID YOU ALL A *GOOD NIGHT...* AND *WARN* YOU THAT I'LL *FLATTEN* ANYONE WHO TRIES TO STOP ME FROM *LEAVING!*

END ACT ONE

ACT TWO

QUICKLY, THE *FIRST* STAGE OF *SOLID* DETECTIVE WORK BEGINS: *DRUDGERY...*

HERE'S A PRETTY COMPREHENSIVE HISTORY OF *THE KNIGHTS OF THE GOLDEN CIRCLE,* ALFRED.

Shhhh!

THEY SEDUCED *MANY* MEN OF SCIENCE TO THEIR *DARK* SIDE. TRULY, AS MY MUM USED TO SAY, MONEY *IS* THE ROOT OF ALL EVIL.

Shhhh!

OH, SHUSH *YOURSELF!* YOU SOUND LIKE A COMMON *RADIATOR!*

AND DEEP *BELOW* THE WAYNE ESTATE IN THE *CAVE* OF BATS, CHEMISTRY BECOMES THE KEY FOR *DETECTIVE #27* AND *DETECTIVE #25...*

GOT IT! WE'VE *ISOLATED* THE DATURA AND THE EMEX SPINOSA POLYGONACEAE!

NOW IT'S *MY* JOB TO SEE IF THEY *MATCH* THE VICTIMS' BLOOD AND TISSUE SAMPLES.

WITHIN HOURS, THE *AUTOPSIES* ARE UNDER WAY...

IDENTICAL!

I CAN'T TELL WHOSE SIDE HE'S REALLY ON...BUT I CAN TELL HE'S BECOME QUITE THE *SKILLED* FORENSIC PATHOLOGIST.

AND INSIDE THE GARAGE THAT ONCE HOUSED DR. THOMAS WAYNE'S *STUTZ BEARCAT* AND *BUGATTI* COLLECTIONS...

EVERY GREAT *DETECTIVE* SHOULD HAVE A GREAT *CAR,* EH, ALFRED?

I'M SIMPLY PLEASED TO SEE THAT YOUR COURSE IN *"AUTOMOTIVE REPAIR"* WAS *NOT* FOR NAUGHT.

SOON, THE ART OF SURVEILLANCE LEADS THE DETECTIVES TO CRIME ALLEY...

HARD TO BELIEVE THIS WAS ONCE PARK ROW, HIGH SOCIETY'S SHOWPLACE.

MY MOTHER WAS RIGHT. IT'S A CRIME HOW THE POLITICIANS LET IT DETERIORATE!

YET ANOTHER SKILL FOR THE EFFECTIVE DETECTIVE: QUESTIONING INFORMANTS...

LOUIE THE LIP! LET'S MAKE A DEAL! I'LL TRADE YOU THE INFO IN YOUR HEAD ABOUT THE KNIGHTS...FOR WHAT'S IN MY FIST!

OH, MAN! YOU-YOU'RE THAT DETECTIVE #27, RIGHT? WORD'S ALREADY OUT ON THE STREET ABOUT YOU!

NO TRADE! YOU CAN HAVE ANYTHING I KNOW... FREE!

LOUIE SPILLED HIS GUTS.

THERE'S AN ACRE OF DATURA GROWING IN GOTHAM'S BOTANICAL GARDENS. THE KNIGHTS AREN'T ON TO IT YET.

IF THEY WERE, THIS GAME WOULD ALREADY BE OVER. LET'S CHECK IT OUT.

PAPER! GET YER PAPER!

EXCLUSIVE IN TODAY'S GOTHAM GAZETTE: POLICE COMMISH GORDON ON MYSTERIOUS CAT-BURGLARIES!

WE'LL TAKE A PAPER, YOUNG MAN. I HAVE TWO CENTS RIGHT HERE... SOMEWHERE.

HEY!

OH!

OOPS! SORRY! I'M REAL CLUMSY!

OW!

HAHAHAHAHAHAHAHAHAHAHA!

ANOTHER DAY PASSES. AS NIGHT FALLS, THE DETECTIVE FAST BECOMING *THE NOCTURNAL KNIGHT* OF GOTHAM CITY *SUITS UP* FOR ACTION...

I HAD A *HUNCH* THE KIDS WOULD LEAD US TO *THE KNIGHTS*, ALFRED, AND IT *PAID OFF!*

NOW WE KNOW *THE KNIGHTS* ARE SOMEHOW TIED TO THE MEDICAL CONVENTION AT *THE VANDERITZ* TONIGHT.

I'LL BE THERE... IN MY NEW *DISGUISE.*

BUT, MASTER BRUCE, YOU AGREED WHEN YOU JOINED *THE SECRET SOCIETY OF DETECTIVES* THERE'D BE *NO* "MYSTERY MAN" HIJINKS TO DISTRACT--

ALFRED! *RELAX!*

DETECTIVE #27 IS THE *REAL ME.* FROM NOW ON, IT'S "BRUCE WAYNE" WHO'LL BE THE *ROLE* I PLAY.

I THINK I CAN MANEUVER MORE EFFECTIVELY IF *GOTHAM* WILL *BUY* ME AS THE PLAYBOY HEIR TO THE FAMILY FORTUNE, WHO JUST RETURNED AFTER STUDYING ABROAD FOR YEARS.

I ALWAYS *KNEW* YOU LOVED "*ZORRO*," BUT COULDN'T YOU BE JUST A *BIT* MORE ORIGINAL?

HA-HA! COME ON, ALFRED. LET'S *CRASH* THIS PARTY.

SATURDAY NIGHT IN *GOTHAM!* THE VANDERITZ HOTEL! THE DRESS IS TUX AND TAILS! THE DINNER IS STEAK AND TAILS!

BUT LEAVE IT TO *DOCTORS* TO SOMEHOW MAKE IT ALL *BORING...*

...AND SO, BASED ON MY *LONG-TERM* RESEARCH INTO DRUGS AND NERVE GASES...

...I CAN PREDICT A GENERATION OF *NEW* DRUGS AND GASES THAT WILL *CONTROL* PEOPLES' *FEARS* AND *PARANOIA*...AND DO SO *WITHOUT* ADVERSE SIDE EFFECTS.

BINGO! OUR *LEADING* SUSPECT...RIGHT OFF THE *BAT!*

GOTHAM MEDICAL CONVENTION 1939

AND THEN, TOO MANY MINUTES LATER, THE LECTURE ENDS AND DINNER IS SERVED...ALONG WITH A *SURPRISE* OR TWO...

WHY, *ALFRED!* Uh... *DR. PENNYWORTH!* SO NICE TO...UH...SEE YOU AGAIN.

41

THAT'S...UH... HUGO STRANGE. DR. STRANGE WAS MY GENETICS PROFESSOR AT MED SCHOOL.

BRILLIANT... POSITIVELY BRILLIANT... BUT MOST ECCENTRIC!

HERE'S THE NEW PLAN...YOU INTRODUCE ME TO STRANGE. I'LL OFFER HIM SOME HUGE WAYNE FOUNDATION RESEARCH GRANT TO WORM MY WAY INTO HIS CONFIDENCE. THEN IF--

EEEEEE

IT... IT'S THE CAT BURGLAR!

LADIES! I WANT YOUR JEWELRY...ALL OF IT...RIGHT NOW! AND I WANT NO RESISTANCE...OR THE GOOD DOCTOR BUYS THE FARM.

OH, YES... ONE MORE THING...

MEOW.

OH, *BRUCE!* I WAS SO WORRIED ABOUT YOU!

DID SHE *HURT* YOU?

JUST STICK CLOSE TO *ME* THE REST OF THE NIGHT AND THAT *CAT* WON'T *DARE* COME NEAR YOU AGAIN!

I WOULDN'T STICK CLOSE TO ANY OF THESE DAMES, MR. WAYNE. WHO'S TO SAY IF ONE OF *THEM* ISN'T REALLY *THE CATWOMAN?!*

DR. STRANGE IS SAFE OUTSIDE. SHALL WE *TAIL* HIM?

PULL THE *CAR* AROUND BACK. LET'S TAKE CARE OF SOME UNFINISHED BUSINESS *FIRST.*

Uh...*EXCUSE ME, LADIES,* BUT DUTY CALLS. THERE'S AN *ELDERLY* WOMAN OVER THERE WHO LOOKS LIKE SHE CAN USE A *HAND.*

BOY SCOUT!

FOP!

MADAME, LET ME *HELP* YOU. ARE YOU ALL RIGHT? YOU SEEM A LITTLE *UNSTEADY.*

ACTUALLY, I DO FEEL ILL AND NEED TO GO HOME. TOO MUCH *EXCITEMENT,* I IMAGINE.

LET *ME* CARRY YOUR PURSE. THAT'S A BIG *BAG* FOR YOU TO MANAGE.

THANK YOU. IT'S NICE TO KNOW THAT *CHIVALRY* ISN'T DEAD, MR.--?

WAYNE. BRUCE WAYNE. AND HERE'S MY CAR AND DRIVER. I *INSIST* YOU LET *ALFRED* DRIVE YOU HOME...UNLESS YOU HAVE YOUR *OWN* CAR AND DRIVER HERE?

NO, I DON'T. THANK YOU, MR. WAYNE. YOU'RE SUCH A *GENTLEMAN!*

44

46

I MISSED SOMETHING HERE. WHY DID SHE CALL ALFRED A "CHARMING LIAR"? HE DIDN'T SAY WORD ONE TO HER. WHAT COULD--

STRANGE! HE'S MAKING HIS MOVE!

HE HAS NO IDEA I'M FOLLOWING HIM.

SAME WAY THE KIDS LED ME TO STRANGE, STRANGE JUST MAY LEAD ME TO THE KING OF THE KNIGHTS.

THIS IS PURE TEXT BOOK SURVEILLANCE. I BET HE--

DAMN!

THERE'S ONLY ONE POSSIBLE REASON YOU'RE TAILING ME, MR. WAYNE. WE TRULY THOUGHT IT WOULD BE IMPOSSIBLE FOR YOU TO FIND OUT.

YOU FORCE OUR HAND. NOW, WE HAVE TO FINISH THE JOB.

FINISH?

THERE'S A CITY AWAITING ITS LONG, PREDESTINED FATE, SO YOU'LL HAVE TO EXCUSE ME.

GOOD EVENING, MR. WAYNE.

...AND GOOD-BYE.

LATER, THAT NIGHT, DEEP WITHIN *THE CAVE OF BATS...*

THIS IS A *NIGHTMARE!* MY MENTOR IS THE POWER BEHIND *THE KNIGHTS OF THE GOLDEN CIRCLE!*

AND THEY HAVE THE *AUDACITY* TO USE THE *MEDICAL SCHOOL* ENDOWED BY *YOUR* FATHER AS THEIR *LAIR!*

THAT'S THE *BAD* NEWS, ALFRED.

THE *GOOD* NEWS, I'M *ASHAMED* TO ADMIT, IS THAT THIS ALL PUTS TO REST A FEW *DOUBTS* I WAS HARBORING ABOUT *YOUR* LOYALTY. I APOLOGIZE FOR THAT.

YOU NEED *NEVER* APOLOGIZE TO ME, MASTER BRUCE.

AND, ALFRED...YOU'RE A SCOTLAND YARD *DETECTIVE* AND A PRACTICING *FORENSIC PATHOLOGIST...*

...SO CUT THE *"MASTER BRUCE"* BALONEY! IT'S *BRUCE*...AND TEACH ME THE LOUSY *SECRET SOCIETY* HANDSHAKE, HUH?

WITH THE *DOOMSDAY CLOCK* TICKING DOWN, DETECTIVES *#27* AND *#25* SPEED TO THE RESEARCH LAB OF *DR. HUGO STRANGE* AT THE GOTHAM CITY MEDICAL SCHOOL'S TEACHING HOSPITAL...

I'D ADVISE *AGAINST* THE FRONT DOOR, MAS--UH... BRUCE.

ANOTHER *SMASHING* SUGGESTION, ALFRED... GRAB THE *GRAPPLING HOOKS* FROM THE BACK SEAT!

BRUCE, YOU KNOW *DR. STRANGE* WAS REPRIMANDED BY THE MED SCHOOL BOARD MORE THAN ONCE FOR HIS *UNAUTHORIZED* EXPERIMENTS ON CON-TROLLING BEHAVIOR THROUGH A COMBINATION OF DRUGS AND HYBRID NERVE GASES.

YOUR *POINT?*

IF HE'S USING SOME *MUTATED* FORM OF *DATURA...* ANY SPORE EXPOSURE COULD SEVERELY *DAMAGE* YOUR NERVOUS SYSTEM...OR *KILL* YOU!

THAT'S WHY *YOU* STAY OUT HERE. YOU'RE THE *ONLY* BACK UP I HAVE.

ANYTHING GOES *WRONG*, CALL IN THE *SECRET SOCIETY!*

I BELIEVE THEY'RE OFF *BURNING* A FIELD OF *DATURA...* BUT I'LL KEEP THAT IN MIND.

52

53

AH! GOOD MORNING, MR. WAYNE.

I HOPE YOUR EXPERIENCE WITH THE *MILDEST* FORM OF *DATURA* WAS NOT TOO UNPLEASANT.

UNFORTUNATELY, YOU'VE BECOME A *NUISANCE*, JEOPARDIZING *75 YEARS* OF PLANNING AND SCIENTIFIC WORK.

DOCTOR STRANGE AND I BOTH FEEL THAT THE *ONE* THING YOU DESERVE, UNDER THE CIRCUMSTANCES, IS AN *EXPLANATION*.

"DESERVE"? WHAT *"CIRCUMSTANCES?"*

WE JOINED *GOTHAM MED* YEARS AGO TO TAP ITS *FUNDING* AND ADVANCED *EQUIPMENT* FOR OUR MIND-ALTERING EXPERIMENTS THAT INDUCED EXTREME *PARANOIA* IN OUR VOLUNTEERS.

I WITNESSED THE *AUTOPSIES* OF SEVERAL OF YOUR *"VOLUNTEERS!"*

WE'RE *KNIGHTS* OF THE *GOLDEN CIRCLE*, EXECUTING PROFESSOR CARR'S DOOMSDAY *PLAN* OF 1864...CONTROLLING PEOPLE WITH THEIR OWN *FEAR*...THEREBY *EXTINGUISHING* THEIR FREEDOM OF *CHOICE!*

CARR KNEW A POPULATION IN *FEAR* COULD *DESTROY* AN ENTIRE CITY.

NOW, WE'LL HELP HIM REACH OUT FROM THE GRAVE... ON THE MOST *IRONIC* DAY OF ALL... EMPOWERING *THE SOUTH* TO RISE AGAIN!

AFTER 75 YEARS, THE *KNIGHTS* ARE READY. GOTHAM FALLS *FIRST!*

FOR *THE NORTH*, IT'S THE *END* OF LIFE, LIBERTY, AND THE PURSUIT OF *SANITY!*

FOR MEN OF *SCIENCE*, YOU'RE BOTH *STUPID* BEYOND BELIEF!

MEASURE YOUR WORDS, MR. WAYNE.

WE'RE UNDER *NO OBLIGATION* TO MAKE YOUR *DEATH* EITHER QUICK OR *PAINLESS!*

54

YOUR MINDS ARE POISONED, PROFESSOR...AND NEITHER OF YOU SEE IT.

AT FIRST, I FIGURED YOU SOLD OUT FOR THE FORTUNE THEY MUST HAVE PAID YOU. THEN, I REALIZED...YOU'RE EXHIBITING CLASSIC SIGNS OF PARANOIA YOURSELVES!

YOUR OWN DATURA TOXINS MUST SEEP THROUGH YOUR PORES! YOU'RE BOTH DELUSIONAL! IF YOU CAN JUST REASON--

A HARD LESSON FOR AN INEXPERIENCED DETECTIVE...WHEN IT COMES TO THE CRIMINALLY INSANE, LOGIC-BASED NEGOTIATION IS, AT BEST, A LONG-SHOT TACTIC...

DON'T THINK WE'RE BLIND TO YOUR LITTLE SECRET SOCIETY, EITHER. WE'VE OUTFOXED IT FOR 75 YEARS.

YOU'LL REMAIN A GUEST IN THIS PADDED CELL IN OUR PSYCHO WARD UNTIL WE DETERMINE YOUR VALUE AS A BARGAINING CHIP.

THAT SHOULD TAKE... OH...TWO HOURS. THEN, WE'LL BE BACK FOR YOUR DATURA OVERDOSE.

MEANWHILE, I'LL LEAVE YOU WITH A FINAL QUESTION TO PONDER...

THIS WAS PROFESSOR CARR'S LITTLE TRADITION WHENEVER A VICTIM WAS ABOUT TO DIE OF FEAR. HOW DOES IT GO AGAIN? AH, YES...

"DID YOU EVER DANCE WITH THE DEVIL BY THE PALE MOONLIGHT?"

55

PURE *SHOCK* NEUTRALIZES THE LINGERING EFFECTS OF THE *DATURA*, ALLOWING BRUCE'S CONTROLLED BREATHING AND CONTRACTING MUSCLES TO EDGE HIM TOWARD *ESCAPE...*

THOSE *SAME* WORDS! WHAT COULD THEY *MEAN?!* WHAT'S THE CONNECTION TO MY *PARENTS'* MURDER?

MUST GET OUT OF HERE *NOW!*

MY MENTOR IN THE ORIENT TAUGHT ME *HOUDINI'S* STRAITJACKET ESCAPE. *NEVER* THOUGHT I'D ACTUALLY *USE* IT IN REAL LIFE!

AND HE TAUGHT ME *ANOTHER* TRICK... IF I CAN JUST *TEAR* OFF THIS SHINY BUCKLE...

I *STILL* THINK OF THIS AS "HYPER-HYPNOSIS." "CLOUDING MEN'S MINDS" ALWAYS SOUNDED LIKE A *WEATHER* REPORT.

HEY, FAT BOY! I'M TUNNELING *OUT* OF HERE! TELL YOUR BOSSES I HADDA *SKIDOO!*

Huh?

THE TOXINS HAVE MADE YOU *NUTSO,* MAC. THERE'S NO WAY YOU CAN TUNNEL--

HEY! WHERE'D YOU GO?!

IT--IT'S *IMPOSSIBLE!* HE'S GONE!

HOLY HAN--

IT *WORKED!* FOR *REAL!* I HYPNOTIZED HIM INTO *NOT* SEEING ME!

AND THOSE *LONG* HOURS I SPENT PRACTICING *PRESSURE POINTS? WORTH* IT! HE COLLAPSED IN A *HEAP!*

NOW TO *TEST* MY *DISGUISE* SKILLS!

...NEVER SHOULD'VE *CUT* SO MANY CLASSES!

ONE HOT SHOWER, ONE HOT MEAL, AND FOUR CUPS OF HOT DETOX TEA LATER, A BLEARY-EYED BRUCE IS JOINED BY ALFRED IN THE CAVE OF BATS FOR ALL-NIGHT RESEARCH IN THE PINKERTON TRADITION...

I FOUND IT, BRUCE! LOOK AT THIS OLD BOOK!

THE PHRASE IS A TWISTED VERSION OF A JOE MILLER PUNCH LINE FROM THE 1800'S. JOSIAH CARR BASTARDIZED IT AS HIS SIGNATURE M.O.

ONLY MY FATHER WOULD HAVE A HUNDRED-YEAR-OLD JOKE BOOK IN HIS COLLECTION! COULD BE OUR BREAK!

THEN "DANCING WITH THE DEVIL IN THE PALE MOONLIGHT" IS AN OBLIQUE REFERENCE TO USING HALLUCINOGENIC "DEVIL'S THORN" AND "DEVIL'S BACKBONE"...

...WHICH BLOSSOM ONLY AT NIGHT, ARE POLLINATED BY BATS, AND--

...INDUCE DEADLY FEAR THROUGH THEIR CROSS-BRED TOXINS!

THE SOCIETY'S NOTES FROM DETECTIVE #4'S WORK WITH GREGOR MENDEL CANNOT BE CONTROVERTED.

THIS CATCH-PHRASE IS, INDEED, A SIGNATURE OF THE DOOMSDAY PLOT!

BUT HOW IN HELL DOES THAT TIE IN TO MY PARENTS' DEATHS?

Hmm. PROFESSOR CRANE WAS HOLDING A BOOK OF ESSAYS... SIGMUND FREUD'S "THEORY OF SEXUALITY, JOKES AND THEIR RELATION TO THE UNCONSCIOUS."

MY DAD HAD A COMPLETE SET OF HIS WORKS... ON THE TOP SHELF...SO I COULDN'T REACH THEM.

PERHAPS YOU'RE STARTING TO READ A BIT TOO MUCH INTO ALL THIS?

FUNNY... THAT'S THE ONE BOOK MISSING FROM THIS SET.

"CURIOUSER AND CURIOUSER..."

57

CLIC

PERHAPS IF WE BOTH HAVE A DECENT NIGHT'S *SLEEP*, WE'LL BE ABLE TO THINK MORE FRESHLY IN THE MORNING.

MAKES SENSE TO ME. LET'S POWER-DOWN THE CAVE...AND ALFRED? FIND OUT IF DR. FREUD IS *STILL* LECTURING IN NEW YORK.

I'LL MAKE THE CALL *FIRST* THING IN THE MORNING.

WE ALREADY *KNOW* THAT PROFESSOR CRANE AND DR. STRANGE ARE THE CURRENT CULPRITS BEHIND *THE KNIGHTS OF THE GOLDEN CIRCLE*.

AND WE KNOW THEY'VE GONE INTO *HIDING*.

WE ALSO KNOW THEIR PLOT IS BASED ON USING A PLANT *TOXIN* CROSS-BRED FOR *75 YEARS*...

...FOR THE SOLE PURPOSE OF WIPING OUT A HUGE NUMBER OF PEOPLE IN A CONTAINED AREA...

...BY MANIPULATING THEIR *FEAR* AND *PANIC* TO *CAUSE* MASSIVE DEATH AND DESTRUCTION..

AND IT WILL HAPPEN *THIS* YEAR ON A DAY THAT JOSIAH CARR FORESAW HIS *SOUTH* RISING AGAIN.

IF, AS CRANE TOLD YOU, IT'S PLANNED FOR THE MOST IRONIC DAY OF ALL, THAT WOULD MOST LIKELY BE--

THE *FOURTH OF JULY!*

BUT *WHERE?*

SO MANY PEOPLE AT *ONE* TIME IN A *LIMITED* AREA?

OPEN ENOUGH FOR THE *WINDS* TO CARRY THE TOXINS. CLOSED ENOUGH TO *BOX* THEM IN TO PREVENT ESCAPE.

PROBABLY TARGETING CITY AND GOVERNMENT OFFICIALS, TOO. Hmmmm... JULY 4TH?

GOTHAM'S YANKEE DOODLE STADIUM! IT MUST HOLD AT *LEAST* 70,000 PEOPLE! JULY 4TH...MAJOR LEAGUE BASEBALL'S *ALL-STAR* GAME!

ALFRED! DO YOU REALIZE WHAT THIS *MEANS?!*

I MOST CERTAINLY *DO*, BRUCE!

THE GAME IS AFOOT!

END ACT TWO

ACT THREE

INDEPENDENCE DAY, 1939... GOTHAM CITY...

A CACOPHONY OF SUMMER CITY SOUNDS...

A SYMPHONY OF SCENTS...HOT DOGS AND ROASTED PEANUTS...

SEDUCING THE CROWD TO THE COMFORTABLE PLEASURES OF AMERICA'S PASTIME...

IT'S REALLY QUITE CHARMING...ACKNOWLEDGING THE YOUNG "BAT BOYS" AND "BAT GIRLS" ON "BAT DAY." NOTHING IN ENGLAND COMPARES WITH THIS.

THEY'RE ALSO HONORING THE PLAYERS FROM THE VERY FIRST ALL-STAR GAME BACK IN '33...

...AS PART OF THE DIAMOND ANNIVERSARY OF THE FIRST BALL GAME EVER PLAYED IN GOTHAM.

EACH ORIGINAL ALL-STAR WILL BE GIVEN A DIAMOND RING.

A DIAMOND TO EACH MAN ON THE BASEBALL DIAMOND? JOLLY GOOD!

TIME TO GET SERIOUS. IS THE REST OF THE SOCIETY HERE?

LOOK, ALFRED! NUMBER 3! THAT'S "THE SULTAN OF SWAT," HIMSELF! IT'S BABE RUTH!

I'M THRILLED. TRULY.

EVERY ALLY WE COULD MUSTER IS PRESENT. SECURITY COULD NOT BE TIGHTER.

C'MON, BOYS! TAKE THE FIELD FOR THE RING CEREMONY! LET'S GO!

HEY, ALFRED! THAT CATCHER LOOK FUNNY TO YOU? HE'S--

--A SHE! AND WHAT A SHE! WHY WOULD--

DIAMONDS? A "CAT-CHER"?

NOT HERE! NOT NOW!

WAIT!

OOOF!

YOU'VE BEEN MY *HERO* SINCE I WAS A KID! I'M *SO* EXCITED! MAY I *PLEASE* HAVE YOUR AUTOGRAPH?

ARE YOU *CRAZY?!* GET *OFFA* ME!

YOU!

YOU HERE TO PLAY *BASEBALL* OR TO SNAG SOME *DIAMONDS?*

ONLY THING I CAN THINK OF RIGHT NOW, MR. WAYNE, IS *SMASHING* A COUPLE OF *BALLS* OVER THE RIGHT FIELD FENCE!

OW!

YOU HAVE A *KNACK* FOR TURNING UP AT THE *WRONG* PLACE AT THE *WRONG* TIME.

AND *SPEAKING* OF GETTING THINGS WRONG, WHAT DID YOU *MEAN* THAT NIGHT... CALLING ALFRED "A CHARMING *LIAR*"?

AS IF YOU DIDN'T KNOW!

I DON'T *KNOW* ANYTHING! MY PARENTS WERE *MURDERED* WHEN I WAS *12* AND I'VE BEEN OVERSEAS EVER *SINCE!*

WHAT DO *YOU* KNOW ABOUT *ALFRED* THAT I DON'T?

"WE'VE *ALL* GOT PROBLEMS, BRUCE. I WAS A *TROUBLED* KID, TOO.

"YOUR *FATHER* WAS MY FAMILY DOCTOR. HE HIRED ME TO WORK AFTER SCHOOL...YOU KNOW...TRYING TO GET ME ON THE *RIGHT PATH*...

"MY JOB WAS 'GOFER'...PICKING UP AND DELIVERING *MEDICAL SUPPLIES* FOR HIS OFFICE.

"EVERY DAY AFTER SCHOOL, *ALFRED* WOULD HAVE A NEW PACKAGE FOR ME TO DROP OFF TO THE *MED SCHOOL*...

"BUT A WEEK LATER, I STARTED FEELING *SCARED*... PARANOID...AND FELL INTO *WORSE* TROUBLE.

"I ASKED ALFRED *WHAT* WAS IN THOSE PACKAGES. HE SAID THEY WERE *SAFE*, BUT *SOMETHING* WAS AFFECTING ME...

"HE WAS A *CHARMING LIAR*... AND I SUFFERED FOR IT...

"I WAS *AFRAID* TO QUIT, BUT WHEN I FINALLY DID, *ALFRED* WAS *FURIOUS!*

"I RAN AWAY FROM HIM... AND FROM *GOTHAM ACADEMY*... THINKING IT WAS MY *ONLY* CHANCE TO SURVIVE..."

WAIT A MINUTE! GOTHAM ACADEMY? I WENT THERE, TOO!

GOD, BRUCE! DON'T *THINK* TOO HARD BECAUSE YOU'RE OBVIOUSLY *NOT* EQUIPPED FOR IT!

I'M *SELINA!*

SELINA? UH... *SELINA!* UH... SELINA *SCHWARTZ?*

NO...*KYLE!* YOU'RE SELINA *KYLE!*

YOU WIN THE KEWPIE DOLL, *SHERLOCK!*

NOW GET THE HELL OFF OF ME!

61

THE DIAMOND-STUDDED CEREMONY ENDS WITHOUT A HITCH. THE STAR-SPANGLED BANNER RESONATES, SIGNALLING THE START OF THE MAIN EVENT...

EVERYONE'S IN PLACE. NOTHING TO REPORT YET. YOU... er...*RESOLVED* THINGS WITH THE YOUNG LADY?

I SUPPOSE.

I TOLD HER I WAS "DETECTIVE 27," REVEALED WHAT I KNEW ABOUT THE *DOOMSDAY PLOT*, ASKED FOR HER *HELP*, THEN LET HER *GO* SO SHE COULD SLIP INTO SOMETHING MORE COMFORTABLE.

I SEE TRAVIS...THE OTHER *SOCIETY* MEMBERS...ROBIN AND HIS BOY COMMANDOS... SELINA...

SOMEONE'S GOING TO SPOT SOMETHING IF *THE KNIGHTS* MAKE THEIR MOVE!

WAIT A TIC... HERE'S SOMETHING *ODD*...THE *BASEBALLS* THAT KID GAVE THE UMP...

THAT'S *NOT* MAJOR LEAGUE REGULATION CROSS-STITCHING ON THEM.

MEANING? *TAMPERED* WITH AND RESEWN?

MOST *PROBABLE* DEDUCTION.

AND IF IT'S *THE KNIGHTS*...IT'S BECAUSE THE BASE-BALLS CONTAIN THE CROSS-BRED *TOXIN*.

WHEN A BATTER HITS THE BALL *HARD* ENOUGH, IT'LL *TEAR* OPEN AND ALL THESE PEOPLE WILL BE IN THE THRALLS OF MASS-INDUCED *HYSTERIA*!

THAT'LL LEAD TO *TRAMPLING*...AND *THOUSANDS* OF PEOPLE *DEAD*!

PLAY BALL!

AS IF IN ANSWER, A HUGE *BAT* FLIES THROUGH THE OPEN WINDOW...

HEY, YOU!

CATCH!

THANKS! I OWE YOU... BIG TIME!

TOO MANY! I'M DONE FOR!

IF WHAT YOU SAID ABOUT THOSE BASEBALLS IS *TRUE,* WE BETTER KNOCK A FEW OF THESE RUBES *OUTTA* THE PARK!

BUT IF YOU'RE JUST SOME *LUNATIC* ...WELL, I'LL BE SPENDING MY RETIREMENT IN *JAIL* FOR ATTEMPTED MANSLAUGHTER!

IT'S ALL *TRUE.* BUT I'M GETTING *TIRED* AND THEY JUST KEEP COMING. *SORRY* I GOT YOU INTO THIS, BABE.

HEY--I ALWAYS *WONDERED* HOW DAVY CROCKETT FELT AT *THE ALAMO!*

HANG ON, #27! HERE COME THE BOY COMMANDOS!

WAHOOOO!

I'LL SECURE THE BASEBALLS, MASTER...UH...! *DON'T WORRY!*

AT *LAST!* THE *CAVALRY!*

HA! IT'S ONLY A *DAME!*

OH, PLEASE! ONE MORE STUPID *LUG* TRAPPED IN THE '20s!

LET ME TEACH YOU ABOUT *SUSAN B. ANTHONY* WHILE I POUND YOU INTO SALT MASH, LUNKHEAD!

CATWOMAN?!

NO, ALFRED. "SELINA!"

SELINA? SELINA! GOOD GOD, CHILD, I--

FOP!

YOU MAY KNOW *EVERY-THING* ABOUT DETECTIVE WORK, *DETECTIVE*, BUT YOU'VE GOT A *LONG* WAY TO GO BEFORE YOU KNOW *ANYTHING* ABOUT *WOMEN!*

WOW! WHO WAS *THAT?!?*

I *THINK*... THAT'S MY NEW *GIRLFRIEND.*

HA! THE *CAT'S* OUTTA THE BAG NOW! SORRY...

AND, PLEASE, THANK *COMMISSIONER GORDON* FOR HIS COOPERATION WITH US IN THIS OPERATION. YOU GENTLEMEN HAVE BEEN *SUPERB!*

ALFRED!

I'VE *CLEARED* YOU WITH THE AUTHORITIES. YOU'LL *NOT* BE DETAINED OR QUESTIONED.

EACH TOXIC BASEBALL HAS BEEN ACCOUNTED FOR AND IS BEING TRANSPORTED TO A *SECURE* GOVERNMENT FACILITY.

ALFRED, THANK YOU. YOU'VE DONE A *GREAT JOB*...BEEN A GREAT *PARTNER.*

I HAVE TO ADMIT I HARBORED SUSPICIONS ABOUT YOU BASED ON THE MOST *INFERIOR* CIRCUMSTANTIAL EVIDENCE.

BY DOUBTING *YOUR* LOYALTY, I ONLY PROVED *MY* DISLOYALTY TO *YOU.*

IT'S ALL JUST PART OF THE GROWING-UP PROCESS, BRUCE.

THE GROWING *TOGETHER* PROCESS.

SOMETIMES CLOSE RELATIVES SQUABBLE AND DOUBT EACH OTHER. *NONE* OF THAT MATTERS. YOU AND I...

...WE'RE *FAMILY.*

HEY, KID--

ALFRED! HANG ON! I'LL GET HELP!

IT'S MY SHOULDER. I'LL LIVE...THOUGH MY CRICKET DAYS MAY WELL BE OVER!

TEND TO THOSE TWO FIRST, BRUCE! I'LL BE FINE.

YOU! I WANT ANSWERS RIGHT NOW OR I'LL TEAR YOU APART WITH MY BARE HANDS!

WHY MY PARENTS? WHY NOT ME?

WERE CRANE AND STRANGE BEHIND THAT MURDER, TOO?

B-BACK OFF, WAYNE... NO MORE! I'LL SPILL...

CRANE GAVE US THE ORDERS.

THE MURDER WAS NEEDED TO ADVANCE THE DOOMSDAY PLAN. IT WAS TO SEEM LIKE A RANDOM BURGLARY GONE BAD.

WE HAD REAL CLEAR INSTRUCTIONS. I WAS TO SHOOT THE DOC.

CHILL WAS TO SHOOT THE MISSUS.

AND BOTH OF US WERE WARNED...LEAVE THE KID ALONE!

CRANE SAID TO ASK THAT QUESTION...IT'S SOME KNIGHTS TRADITION. I DON'T EVEN KNOW WHAT IT MEANS.

IT MAKES NO SENSE! WHY LET ME LIVE? YOU WERE LEAVING AN EYEWITNESS TO MURDER!

I DUNNO... MAYBE CRANE DIDN'T WANNA ICE A KID.

RIGHT. EXCEPT FOR MAYBE 30,000 OF THEM HERE AT THE STADIUM TODAY. HOGWASH!

WHERE IS HE? STRANGE, TOO!

ON THEIR WAY TO THE NEW YORK WORLD'S FAIR. NATIONAL CASH REGISTER PAVILION.

SWEAR TO GOD!

BRUCE! I FORGOT TO TELL YOU ABOUT THE CABLE!

DR. FREUD IS STILL IN NEW YORK...THE ASTOR HOTEL...

EXIT

BOOK THESE TWO, ALFRED. THEN BOOK FREUD FOR BREAKFAST TOMORROW AT EIGHT...

IT'S TIME FOR SOME ANSWERS!

A NEW DAWN AND A NEW *HOPE*...

YOUR *DEDUCTIONS* BASED UPON THE FACTS AS WELL AS MY THEORY OF *JOKES* AND THE UNCONSCIOUS ARE QUITE *SOUND*, DETECTIVE.

MEANING *WHAT*, DR. *FREUD*?

IF WHAT YOU SAY IS *TRUE*, I CAN CONCLUDE JOSIAH CARR WAS *OBSESSED* WITH HIS PREDILECTION FOR *JOKES* AND THE SHEER IRONY OF TYING EVENTS OF *DEATH* AND SADNESS TO HIS TWISTED *PUNCH LINES*.

AND NOW, JONATHAN CRANE AND HUGO STRANGE ARE TWO *COPYCATS*, EQUALLY *WARPED*, WITH SOME *COMPELLING* NEED TO EMULATE *CARR'S* MINDSET IN ORDER TO EXECUTE *HIS* PLAN OF ATTACK?

YES, EXCEPT... CARR'S "JOKE" WAS TO BE ON *THE NORTH*...

...HOWEVER, IT'S *OBVIOUS* TO ME THAT CRANE AND STRANGE HAVE MADE IT *PERSONAL*. THEIR *FINAL* JOKE MAY YET BE ON *YOU*, DETECTIVE. BE *ALERT*.

I CAN HANDLE THE *JOKES*, DOCTOR, JUST *NOT* THE *DATURA* AND THE *FEAR* IT SPARKS.

"FEAR" IS A *RESPONSE*, SIR...WHETHER *REAL* OR *FALSELY* PERCEIVED.

A *STRONG MIND*, SHARPLY FOCUSED ON THE REALITY OF THE SITUATION, *WILL CONQUER* ANY *IRRATIONAL* FEAR, *DESPITE* THE EFFECTS OF A DRUG OR TOXIN IMPACTING THE NERVOUS SYSTEM.

THANKS FOR YOUR HELP. YOU *KNEW* YOU MIGHT BE PLACING YOUR *LIFE* IN JEOPARDY BY MEETING WITH ME--

...AND I PLAN TO *REMAIN* ALIVE LONG ENOUGH TO ANALYZE THE *TRAUMA* YOU SUFFERED BY WITNESSING YOUR PARENTS' *MURDER* AS A CHILD. *FASCINATING!*

I'M *CONFOUNDED* IT HASN'T RESULTED IN SERIOUS *SCHIZOPHRENIC* TENDENCIES!

YOU MOST CERTAINLY *PUZZLE* ME, DETECTIVE. INDEED...

WITH TIME RUNNING OUT, *DESTINY* CALLS TO DETECTIVE #27...

...AND AS *MAYOR* OF NEW YORK, IT'S MY GREAT *HONOR* TO INTRODUCE THE *PRESIDENT* OF THE UNITED STATES... *FRANKLIN DELANO ROOSEVELT!*

THANK YOU, MAYOR LAGUARDIA! I'M DELIGHTED TO BE BACK AT THE WORLD'S FAIR TO HONOR A NEW KIND OF AMERICAN HERO-- A ROLE MODEL FOR OUR CHILDREN AND AN INSPIRATION TO OUR SERVICEMEN--

HE'S AN IDEAL FOR PEOPLE EVERYWHERE WHO BELIEVE IN TRUTH, JUSTICE, AND THE AMERICAN WAY!

HE'S SUPERMAN!

THAT FELLOW SHOULD BE PITIED, NOT COSTUMED AND PARADED BEFORE THESE GAWKERS LIKE SOME TOD BROWNING FREAK OF NATURE.

WITHIN THE NATIONAL CASH REGISTER PAVILION IS THE ULTIMATE C.P.A. AMUSEMENT PARK-- A SURREALISTIC MAX FLEISCHER WONDER-WORLD FOR PENCIL-PUSHERS, BEAN-COUNTERS, AND NUMBER-CRUNCHERS...

HAVE TO SEARCH *FAST!* IF THEY SPOT *ME* BEFORE I SPOT *THEM,* THE DATURA SPORES ARE GONNA *FLY!*

CAN'T BE... CAN'T...

I HOPE *ALFRED* AT LEAST TAUGHT YOU *NOT* TO *JUDGE* PEOPLE, BRUCE. I DID HAVE *COMPELLING* REASONS TO DO WHAT I DID.

"THE *KNIGHTS* RECRUITED ME THROUGH MY *MENTOR* IN MEDICINE.

"THERE WERE *NO* EMPTY PROMISES...ONLY SATCHELS OF NEGOTIABLE INSTRUMENTS, BEARER BONDS, AND GOLD BULLION...

"I *QUICKLY* ROSE THROUGH THE RANKS OF THE DOCTORS AND PROFESSORS COMPRISING THE CONSPIRATORS IN THEIR *DOOMSDAY* PLAN.

"PERHAPS MY WELL-DESERVED *EGO* WAS A FACTOR IN MY ASCENDANCY TO POWER...

"I CHANNELED *MASSIVE* FUNDING INTO INCREASING THE *TECHNOLOGY* OF THE MED SCHOOL.

"IT WAS THE *ONLY* WAY WE COULD SYNTHESIZE THE CROSS-BRED TOXINS IN *TIME* TO FULFILL THE *PLAN* AND DO SO UNDER COVER.

BUILDING FOR THE FUTURE...THE NEW GOTHAM CITY MEDICAL SCHOOL AND TEACHING HOSPITAL

"THE *MONEY* AND THE *TECHNOLOGY* CONTINUED TO ATTRACT THE *BRIGHTEST* MINDS TO OUR CAUSE...OH, MAYBE AIDED FROM TIME TO TIME BY SOME CAREFULLY CONTROLLED FEAR INDUCTION.

"THEY *NEVER* KNEW WHAT HIT THEM. WE HAD A *ZERO* REFUSAL RATE TO OUR RECRUITMENT EFFORTS.

"LAUNDERING MONEY THROUGH THE MED SCHOOL, I ALWAYS FEARED DETECTION.

"INSTEAD, THE DELUDED BUREAUCRATS *NAMED* THE DAMN PLACE FOR ME AND MADE ME THEIR *'MAN OF THE YEAR!'*

MAN OF THE YEAR
1929

"EVEN AFTER MY *'DEATH,'* I CONTINUED MOVING MONEY FROM SUPPOSEDLY UNTOUCHABLE ESTATE TRUSTS AND INTO THE *KNIGHTS'* COFFERS...*"

YES, SIR. THOSE FUNDS *WILL* BE DIVERTED...AND *UNTRACEABLE.*

MY *USUAL* FEE? CREDITED TO THE MUNICH ACCOUNT? EXCELLENT!

MY GOD! DAD! IT REALLY IS YOU! BUT...I SAW YOU DIE!

...I SAW YOU DIE...

MOM! IS MOM--?

NO!

THIS *ISN'T* SOME FRANK CAPRA MOVIE! I'M THE *HEAD* OF THE KNIGHTS OF THE GOLDEN CIRCLE! I'M YOUR *ENEMY!*

I *DON'T* UNDERSTAND. I HAVE SO MANY *QUESTIONS.* HOW DID YOU *SURVIVE* THE SHOOTING? AND SELINA KYLE! DID YOU--

SELINA KYLE?! WHAT'S THAT BRAT HAVE TO DO WITH *ANYTHING?* I USED HER AS A RUNNER TO DELIVER *TOXINS* TO THE *KNIGHTS.*

AND I *DIDN'T* SURVIVE THE SHOOTING...I *ORCHESTRATED* IT!

SHE WAS *PERFECT*-- NOT AT ALL SUSPICIOUS...VERY *EXPENDABLE...*

NO, YOU *DIDN'T!* YOU JUST *ADMITTED* THE KNIGHTS USED TOXINS TO RECRUIT PEOPLE.

THAT'S WHAT THEY'VE DONE TO *YOU!* THEY'VE *IMPAIRED YOUR MIND* THROUGH FEAR INDUCTION. YOU *DON'T* REALIZE--

YOU DON'T REALIZE! FACE *REALITY,* BRUCE!

I ARRANGED MY *OWN* "MURDER" SO I COULD CONVENIENTLY *DISAPPEAR* FROM PUBLIC VIEW AND *ENTIRELY* DEVOTE MYSELF TO CARRYING OUT THE *DOOMSDAY PLAN.*

I *HAD* TO SACRIFICE MARTHA. SHE WAS *SMART* AND GETTING *CLOSE* TO FIGURING OUT MY *DOUBLE LIFE.* SHE'D *NEVER* HAVE STOOD FOR IT.

82

HE'S GOOD. VERY, *VERY* GOOD. I DON'T THINK I CAN *STOP* HIM.

HE'S *STILL* MY FLESH AND BLOOD...I *DON'T* WANT TO *KILL* HIM...

BUT IF IT'S HIM *OR* MY "WORK"...I HAVE TO CHOOSE MY *WORK*!

ENOUGH!

NO MORE!

YOU *DIDN'T* CONSIDER THE *CONSEQUENCES* OF YOUR ACTIONS, *SON.*

YOU LEAVE ME *NO CHOICE.* *FAILURE IS NOT AN OPTION!*

DAD! YOU HAVE TO THINK *CLEARLY,* OKAY? YOU *CAN'T* LET THOSE *SPORES* LOOSE ON THE *PRESIDENT!*

IF SOME COUNTRY SHOULD MAKE A MOVE AGAINST AMERICA, A *FEAR-STRICKEN* F.D.R. COULD RESULT IN OUR *DEFEAT!*

REASON IT OUT!

REASON? THE *DOOMSDAY PLAN* IS MY *VERY* "*RAISON D'ETRE,*" SONNY-BOY!

IRONIC... *YOU'VE* BEEN MINE FOR THE *LAST TEN YEARS!*

AND THERE GOES THE PRESIDENT'S *LAST BEST* CHANCE OF PROTECTION!

DON'T DO IT, DAD!

AND DR. THOMAS WAYNE...ONCE AGAIN...IS DEAD!

HE-HE'S GONE! TWICE DEAD... THIS TIME AT MY HAND!

FREUD WAS RIGHT. IN THE END, THE JOKE WAS ON ME!

BRUCE! BRUCE!! THANK GOD YOU'RE ALL RIGHT!

AND YOU?

MY SHOULDER WILL HEAL FAR MORE QUICKLY THAN YOUR HEART, I'M AFRAID.

I RECOGNIZED HIM AT ONCE! I CAN'T COMPREHEND IT. YOU MUST EXPLAIN HOW--

ALFRED... THERE IS NO EXPLANATION.

HE WAS BEHIND IT ALL. HE MURDERED MY MOTHER...MURDERED MY SOUL.

THEY'RE HERE TO TAKE ME IN...

NO. I STILL HAVE MY CONNECTIONS. YOU'LL BE QUESTIONED LATER. CONSIDER IT ONE OF THE BENEFITS OF THE SECRET SOCIETY OF DETECTIVES!

YOU DID IT, BRUCE! SAVED TWO CITIES AND THE PRESIDENT! NOT A BAD DAY'S WORK!

I COULDN'T TELL...THAT GUY... WAS IT REALLY YOUR FATHER?

WHY DON'T WE ALL CONTAIN OUR CURIOSITY UNTIL LATER? THIS MAN NEEDS TO REST!

IT WAS HIM, LEE. HE DECIDED HIS WORK... AND THE POWER AND MONEY...WAS WORTH MORE TO HIM THAN THE LIVES OF HIS WIFE AND CHILD.

I CAN'T BELIEVE IT WAS THE SAME TOM WAYNE I KNEW!

HE WAS A DEMON!

I CHOOSE TO BELIEVE HE WAS A VICTIM.

GREED...EGO... MAY HAVE PULLED HIM DOWN, BUT THE TOXINS... NO MATTER HOW THEY WERE CONTAINED OVER THE YEARS... MUST HAVE SEEPED THROUGH HIS PORES...AFFECTED HIS MIND...

NO, DR. THOMAS WAYNE DIED IN 1929. THERE'LL BE NO RECORD OF A RESURRECTION IN 1939 TO SULLY HIS GOOD NAME.

HAVE THE SECRET SOCIETY USE ITS "INFLUENCE" TO MAKE CERTAIN OF THAT.

END OF STORY?

YES... END OF STORY.

DETECTIVE #27 ALSO DIED TODAY. THE DOOMSDAY PLOT IS OVER. THERE'S NO LONGER A REASON FOR THE SECRET SOCIETY TO EXIST.

OPEN YOUR EYES, BRUCE! THERE'S INCREASING FIFTH COLUMN ACTIVITY IN AMERICA... HATRED SPEWING FROM THE BUND!

MORE THAN EVER, THIS COUNTRY NEEDS YOU AND THE SECRET SOCIETY! IT NEEDS HEROES!

CAN ONE PERSON REALLY MAKE A DIFFERENCE?

TODAY, YOU'RE LIVING PROOF OF THAT, BRUCE. NOW JUST IMAGINE 27 PEOPLE WORKING IN CONCERT... LIKE 48 STATES WORKING AS ONE UNION.

YOUNG MAN! DETECTIVE #27, ISN'T IT?

MR. PRESIDENT! YES, SIR.

YOUR FELLOW DETECTIVES INFORMED ME OF WHAT WAS TRANSPIRING HERE TODAY. COULD HAVE BEEN A TERRIBLE BLOW TO THE AMERICAN PEOPLE!

YOU SOUND LIKE THE ALLAN PINKERTON OF THE 20TH CENTURY! GOOD WORK!

MY FATHER WAS BEHIND THIS PLOT. IT WAS MY RESPONSIBILITY TO END HIS THREAT.

I MAY HAVE HELPED THE COUNTRY, BUT I'M AFRAID I FAILED TO HELP HIM...AND HE SO NEEDED MY HELP.

DON'T YOU BE AFRAID! NOT OF FAILURE! NOT OF ANYTHING! THAT'S WHAT KEEPS AMERICA STRONG! THE ONLY THING YOU HAVE TO FEAR, DETECTIVE, IS FEAR, ITSELF!

I WAS 16 WHEN I HEARD YOU SAY THAT OVER THE RADIO. IT GAVE ME COURAGE DURING SOME DARK DAYS...AS IT DOES AGAIN TODAY.

WORDS OF WISDOM FROM THE *PRESIDENT*.

AND?

BETTER TEACH ME THE SECRET HANDSHAKE, 26!

AT THE NEXT MEETING, 27! SEE YOU THERE! AND *DON'T* FORGET TO BRING YOUR "ORPHAN ANNIE" DE-CODER RING!

EXCELLENT DECISION...JOINING UP AND ALL THAT!

TIME FOR *ANOTHER* ONE. MISS KYLE IS ANXIOUSLY AWAITING YOUR RETURN TO *GOTHAM*.

MY *FIRST* REAL ROMANCE...MAYBE A BIT ON THE DARKER, *KINKIER* SIDE OF ROMANCE...BUT *ROMANCE*, NONETHELESS, Eh?

SHE MAY BE *THE CATWOMAN*, BUT *YOU*, SIR, ARE ONE LUCKY *DOG*!

I AM. BECAUSE OF *YOU*, ALFRED. *YOU'VE* BEEN MY FATHER. *YOU* WERE ALWAYS THERE FOR ME...GAVE ME MY *DIRECTION* IN LIFE. AND *NOW*, YOU'RE ALL THE FAMILY I HAVE *LEFT* IN THE WORLD.

MY "FELLOW DETECTIVE"... MY "SON"...

YOU'RE A DOCTOR. YOU SPEAK *LATIN*. I KNOW "CARPE DIEM" MEANS "SEIZE THE DAY". BUT MY FATHER'S *LAST WORDS* TO ME WERE "CARPE NOX."

"SEIZE THE NIGHT".

WHAT DID HE MEAN BY THAT? ADVICE? A *WARNING*? ONE LAST *PUNCH LINE* TO CHALLENGE ME?

I DON'T KNOW WHY HE SAID THAT TO YOU, BRUCE, BUT I *DO* KNOW YOU HAVE YOUR *WHOLE* LIFE AHEAD OF YOU TO SEEK THE *ANSWER*.

SO "CARPE NOX", DETECTIVE #27...

..."CARPE NOX"!

AND FOR BRUCE WAYNE AND DR. ALFRED PENNYWORTH...*DETECTIVE #27* AND *DETECTIVE #25*, RESPECTIVELY...A MILLION *POSSIBILITIES* LIE AHEAD AS A *NEW* NIGHT BEGINS TO FALL ON THE CITY...

THE END

FOOTNOTES TO HISTORY

DETECTIVE #27, LIKE *RAGTIME*, *THE ALIENIST*, *THE AMAZING ADVENTURES OF KAVALIER & CLAY*, AND *CARTER BEATS THE DEVIL*, IS ABOUT A FICTIONAL CHARACTER ENTWINED WITH REAL PEOPLE WHILE MINGLING IN REAL EVENTS OF HISTORY. HISTORY BUFFS, THEREFORE, MIGHT FIND THEIR READING OF THIS GRAPHIC NOVEL ENRICHED BY THE FOLLOWING NOTES AS TO WHO AND WHAT IN THIS TALE WERE BASED ON FACT. GET THE FULL, TRUE STORY BY EXPLORING EACH OF THE FOLLOWING ON THE INTERNET OR AT YOUR LOCAL LIBRARY:

PAGE 1. ABRAHAM LINCOLN (1809-1865)- 16TH PRESIDENT OF THE UNITED STATES.

PAGE 1. ALLAN PINKERTON (1819-1884)- FOUNDER OF THE PINKERTON DETECTIVE AGENCY AND THE U.S. SECRET SERVICE. FOUGHT THE KNIGHTS OF THE GOLDEN CIRCLE, SMASHING THEIR 1861 PLOT TO ASSASSINATE LINCOLN.

PAGE 1. "THE PRESIDENT'S HOUSE"- A COMMON PHRASE USED TO DESCRIBE 1600 PENNSYLVANIA AVENUE UNTIL TEDDY ROOSEVELT IN 1901 OFFICIALLY CHRISTENED IT "THE WHITE HOUSE."

PAGE 1. MARY TODD LINCOLN (1818-1882)- VOLATILE WIFE OF ABRAHAM LINCOLN.

PAGE 1. MAJOR HENRY RATHBONE (1837-1911) AND MISS CLARA HARRIS (1834-1883)- THE ENGAGED COUPLE INVITED TO JOIN THE LINCOLNS IN THE PRESIDENTIAL BOX AT FORD'S THEATRE. HE FAILED TO STOP OR CAPTURE JOHN WILKES BOOTH AND SLOWLY DESCENDED INTO MADNESS. HE MARRIED CLARA, HAD A FAMILY WITH HER, AND BRUTALLY MURDERED HER IN 1883.

PAGE 2. CONSTABLE JOHN PARKER'S THIRST, COUPLED WITH THE LACK OF JURIS-DICTION OF THE NEW U.S. SECRET SERVICE IN WASHINGTON DC, DID LEAD TO THE SUCCESSFUL ASSASSINATION OF ABRAHAM LINCOLN BY JOHN WILKES BOOTH AT FORD'S THEATRE ON APRIL 14, 1865.

PAGE 4. THE ROCKING CHAIR IN WHICH LINCOLN WAS SITTING WHEN HE WAS ASSASSINATED WAS PURCHASED BY HENRY FORD AT AUCTION IN 1929 AND MAY BE FOUND TODAY AT THE HENRY FORD MUSEUM IN DEARBORN, MICHIGAN.

PAGE 7. IN 1929, THE S.S. MAURITANIA OF THE CUNARD LINE WAS SAILING BETWEEN NEW YORK CITY AND LIVERPOOL.

PAGE 8. THE KNIGHTS OF THE GOLDEN CIRCLE- AN EXTREMIST ORGANIZATION OF SOUTHERN SECESSIONISTS INFILTRATED BY PINKERTON'S "PINKS," WHO FOILED ITS 1861 PLOT TO ASSASSINATE LINCOLN AS WELL AS ITS OTHER ESPIONAGE ACTIVITIES.

PAGE 9. "EXPERIMENTS IN PLANT HYBRIDIZATION" BY GREGOR MENDEL (1822-1884) WOULD LEAD TO A NEW WORLD UNDERSTANDING OF GENETICS. MENDEL'S WORK WAS FINALLY PUBLISHED IN 1866 BUT RECEIVED NO ATTEN-TION UNTIL 1900.

PAGE 9. JOE MILLER'S JOKE BOOK- OFTEN MENTIONED AS ABE LINCOLN'S FAVORITE BOOK. THIS WAS THE FIRST ENGLISH LANGUAGE JOKE BOOK, ORIGINALLY PUBLISHED AFTER MILLER'S DEATH, IN 1738.

PAGE 12. CHARLES DARWIN (1809-1882)- THIS NATURALIST STUDIED PLANTS AND ANIMALS, LEADING HIM TO ADVANCE THE THEORY OF EVOLUTION AND THE PROCESS HE CALLED "NATURAL SELECTION."

PAGE 14. KATE WARNE – MRS. WARNE JOINED THE PINKERTON DETECTIVE AGENCY IN 1856, BECOMING THE FIRST FEMALE DETECTIVE IN THE U.S. SHE MOVED ON TO THE U.S. SECRET SERVICE FORMED BY PINKERTON AND WORKED UNDERCOVER, POSING AS A SOUTHERN BELLE TO GAIN INFORMATION ON CONFEDERATE TROOP MOVEMENTS.

PAGE 14. WILLIAM PINKERTON- SON OF ALLAN PINKERTON, RECRUITED AT AGE 16 TO JOIN HIS FATHER'S DETECTIVE AGENCY AND SECRET SERVICE, WAS AN EFFECTIVE UNDERCOVER OPERATIVE, SPY, AND FIELD AGENT. AFTER HIS FATHER'S DEATH, HE AND HIS BROTHER ROBERT RAN THE AGENCY.

PAGE 19. THE PENNSYLVANIA LIMITED- ONE OF SEVERAL TRAINS CONNECTING CHICAGO AND NEW YORK CITY IN THE 1880s.

PAGE 19. THEODORE ROOSEVELT (1858-1919)- 26TH PRESIDENT OF THE U.S. WHO, IN 1884, WAS THE 26-YEAR-OLD MEMBER OF THE N.Y. STATE ASSEMBLY AND CHAIRMAN OF THE COMMITTEE ON CITIES. HIS FIRST CHILD HAD BEEN BORN ON FEBRUARY 12TH AND HIS WIFE AND MOTHER HAD BOTH DIED ON FEBRUARY 14TH OF THAT SAME YEAR.

PAGE 20. IN AN ATTEMPT TO RAISE SUFFICIENT FUNDS TO ERECT AND MAINTAIN FRANCE'S GIFT OF A STATUE OF "LIBERTY ENLIGHTENING THE WORLD," JUST THE HAND HOLDING THE TORCH WAS SENT AHEAD TO NEW YORK CITY WHERE IT WAS PLACED ON DISPLAY IN MADISON SQUARE. PASSERSBY COULD CLIMB INSIDE IT AS A PREVIEW OF THE FULL STATUE TO COME. IN FUTURE YEARS, ITS NAME WAS COMMONLY SHORTENED TO "THE STATUE OF LIBERTY."

PAGE 20. IN 1884, POLO WAS OUT AND BASEBALL WAS IN AT THE ORIGINAL POLO GROUNDS IN CENTRAL PARK BETWEEN 5TH AVENUE AND 6TH AVENUE AT 110TH STREET TO 112TH STREET. THE N.Y. METROPOLITANS PLAYED ON THE SOUTHWEST FIELD, WHILE THE NEW YORKS (EVENTUALLY CALLED THE GIANTS) PLAYED ON THE SOUTHEAST FIELD.

PAGE 20. "OLD SLEUTH" WAS A HUGELY POPULAR DIME NOVEL DETECTIVE BEGINNING IN 1872 IN "FIRESIDE COMPANION" AND "OLD SLEUTH LIBRARY."

PAGE 22. THE CELTIC, ONE OF THE GREAT SHIPS OF THE WHITE STAR LINE CON-NECTING LIVERPOOL WITH NEW YORK CITY, WOULD BE INVOLVED IN 1887 IN AN INFAMOUS COLLISION WITH ANOTHER WHITE STAR SHIP, THE BRITANNIC, 300 MILES OFF THE COAST OF SANDY HOOK, NJ.

PAGE 22. TEDDY ROOSEVELT WOULD, IN FACT, BE APPOINTED POLICE COMMISSIONER OF NEW YORK CITY BY MAYOR STRONG IN 1895.

PAGE 24. ROBERT FROST (1874-1963)- AUTHOR OF THE POEM "THE ROAD NOT TAKEN."

PAGE 29. DELMONICO'S RESTAURANT WAS TEDDY ROOSEVELT'S FAVORITE, LOCATED ON 5TH AVENUE AND 26TH STREET ON MADISON SQUARE. OWNER CHARLES DELMONICO'S DEATH — IN 1884, AS WELL — WAS REPORTED AS "UNEXPECTED AND VERY ODD."

PAGE 29. "LOBSTER WENBERG" WAS CREATED IN 1876 BY BEN WENBERG AND SERVED EXCLUSIVELY AT DELMONICO'S UNTIL HE GOT INTO AN ARGUMENT WITH CHARLES DELMONICO SOME MONTHS LATER. AN ANGRY CHARLES, DETERMINED TO STRIP BEN OF CREDIT, REVERSED THE LETTERS "W" AND "N" IN "WENBERG" AND THUS, "LOBSTER NEWBERG" WAS BORN.

PAGE 29. DATURA- VERY DANGEROUS, VERY POWERFUL, VERY BEAUTIFUL PLANT CAPABLE OF INDUCING HALLUCINATIONS AND NIGHTMARES AND, IN SUFFICIENT DOSAGE, PERMANENT INSANITY OR DEATH. SEE ALSO EMEX SPINOSA POLYGONACEAE/DEVIL'S THORN/DEVIL'S BACKBONE/THORN APPLE.

PAGE 30. THE DAKOTA- THE FIRST GRAND APARTMENT BUILDING ON NEW YORK CITY'S UPPER WEST SIDE OPENED ITS DOORS IN 1884 ON 72ND STREET OVERLOOKING CENTRAL PARK.

PAGE 32. CARL SANDBURG (1878-1967)- AUTHOR OF THE POEM "THEY WILL SAY."

PAGE 39. "GINGER SNAP" WAS A COMIC PAGE CREATED BY BOB KANE WHICH ACTUALLY DEBUTED IN MORE FUN COMICS #36 (OCTOBER 1938) AND APPEARED IN NEW YORK WORLD'S FAIR COMICS 1939.

PAGE 50. 1934 BROUGHT THE WORLD THE PULP MAGAZINE, "OPERATOR #5" BY CURTIS STEELE (REAL NAME: FREDERICK DAVIS), AND THE COMIC STRIP "SECRET AGENT X-9" BY FORMER PINKERTON DETECTIVE DASHIELL HAMMETT AND ARTIST ALEX RAYMOND.

PAGE 52. THAT "PAPER-HANGER IN BERLIN" EVENTUALLY BECAME DER FUEHRER, ADOLF HITLER.

PAGE 54. "THREE ESSAYS ON THE THEORY OF SEXUALITY, JOKES AND THEIR RELATION TO THE UNCONSCIOUS" BY SIGMUND FREUD WAS PUBLISHED IN 1905 AND CONSIDERED BY DR. FREUD TO BE HIS MOST IMPORTANT WORK NEXT TO "THE INTERPRETATION OF DREAMS." FREUD DIED IN 1939.

PAGE 59. BABE RUTH, "THE SULTAN OF SWAT," PLAYED IN MAJOR LEAGUE BASEBALL'S FIRST ALL-STAR GAME IN 1933. HIS UNIFORM NUMBER WAS "3". THE 1939 ALL-STAR GAME WAS PLAYED AT YANKEE STADIUM.

PAGE 73. THE HOTEL ASTOR- IN TIMES SQUARE, IT WAS A PALACE FOR THE ELITE. THE ASTOR BAR WAS A FAMOUS HANGOUT FOR CELEBRITIES, POLITI-CIANS, AND POWERFUL MEN IN BIG BUSINESS.

PAGE 74. THE NEW YORK WORLD'S FAIR OF 1939 AND '40 TOOK PLACE WHERE THE 1964-65 WORLD'S FAIR, SHEA STADIUM, THE NATIONAL TENNIS CENTER, AND FLUSHING MEADOWS PARK HAVE SINCE TAKEN ROOT. WHILE THERE WAS A NATIONAL CASH REGISTER PAVILION AT THE '39 FAIR, IT WAS NOT IN THE SHAPE OF A GIANT CASH REGISTER. THAT PARTICULAR BUILDING WAS ACTUALLY THE NATIONAL CASH REGISTER PAVILION AT THE SAN FRANCISCO WORLD'S FAIR OF 1939. "SUPERMAN DAY" AT THE NEW YORK WORLD'S FAIR IN 1939 WAS PART OF A PROMOTIONAL TIE-IN TO DC COMICS' PUBLICATION OF NEW YORK WORLD'S FAIR COMICS 1939, WHICH FEATURED SUPERMAN, BATMAN, AND OTHER DC HEROES. RAY MIDDLETON WAS THE ACTOR PORTRAYING THE MAN OF STEEL THAT DAY. "SUPERMAN DAY" WAS REPEATED ON JULY 3, 1940 IN CONNECTION WITH DC'S PUBLICATION OF NEW YORK WORLD'S FAIR COMICS 1940.

PAGE 74. MAYOR FIORELLO LAGUARDIA (1882-1947)- MAYOR OF NEW YORK CITY DURING THE 1939-'40 WORLD'S FAIR,

PAGE 74. FRANKLIN DELANO ROOSEVELT (1882-1945)- 32ND PRESIDENT OF THE UNITED STATES WHO, IN 1941, WOULD MAKE A LEGENDARY SPEECH ABOUT THE "FOUR FREEDOMS," WHICH WOULD INCLUDE "THE FREEDOM FROM FEAR."

PAGE 74. TOD BROWNING- MOVIE DIRECTOR OF "FREAKS" AND THE ORIGINAL "DRACULA."

PAGE 93. THANKS TO OVALTINE, KIDS COULD ORDER A "LITTLE ORPHAN ANNIE" DECODER RING TO DECIPHER SECRET MESSAGES BROADCAST DURING EACH EPISODE OF HER RADIO ADVENTURES.